Descartes' Conversation with Burman

Descartes'
Conversation with
Burman

*Translated with Introduction
and Commentary by*

John Cottingham

CLARENDON PRESS · OXFORD
1976

Oxford University Press, Ely House, London W. 1

GLASGOW NEW YORK TORONTO MELBOURNE WELLINGTON
CAPE TOWN IBADAN NAIROBI DAR ES SALAAM LUSAKA ADDIS ABABA
DELHI BOMBAY CALCUTTA MADRAS KARACHI LAHORE DACCA
KUALA LUMPUR SINGAPORE HONG KONG TOKYO

ISBN 0 19 824528 9

Printed in Great Britain by
Richard Clay (The Chaucer Press) Ltd
Bungay, Suffolk

ACKNOWLEDGEMENTS

I AM grateful to Dr. L. J. Beck, Professor Harry Frankfurt, and Professor Bernard Williams for their helpful criticisms on various points. My chief debt is to my former supervisor, Dr. Anthony Kenny, who has encouraged me in this project from the beginning and has given me a great deal of valuable advice and criticism on both the Translation and the Commentary.

CONTENTS

ABBREVIATIONS

AT   *Œuvres de Descartes*, publiées par Ch Adam et P. Tannery (12 vols. Paris: Cerf, 1897–1913; repr. Paris: Vrin, 1957–).

HR   *The Philosophical Works of Descartes*, rendered into English by Elizabeth Haldane and G. R. T. Ross (2 vols. Cambridge: Cambridge University Press, 1911; repr. 1969).

AG   *Descartes, Philosophical Writings*, a selection translated by Elizabeth Anscombe and Peter Thomas Geach (London: Nelson, 1969).

K   *Descartes, Philosophical Letters*, translated by Anthony Kenny (Oxford: Clarendon Press, 1970).

Note: References to HR, AG, and K are given for the reader's convenience, but translations are my own unless otherwise stated. All other works quoted are referred to by the author's or editor's name in SMALL CAPITALS, and are listed in full in the Bibliography.

INTRODUCTION

I

THE *Conversation with Burman* is the report of a philosophical
interview with one of the world's greatest philosophers.
This alone is enough to place it in a genre of its own and to
give it a unique interest. For the *Conversation* provides what
the student of Philosophy so often yearns for in vain, the
opportunity to see a philosopher being closely questioned
about key aspects of his published work. To describe the
Conversation as an 'interview' is perhaps slightly misleading,
since the word, in its modern connotation, conjures up a
picture of the radio or television confrontation. In one way,
this is appropriate enough: the *Conversation* certainly has the
immediacy and informality of a modern broadcast interview. But on the other hand, we tend to think of the
interview as something essentially lightweight. Of course
there can be, and have been, successful broadcast interviews
with philosophers. But, even at their best, such encounters
do not seem to do very much more than scratch the surface,
philosophically speaking. A philosopher may give a general
assessment of his work, or may reply to some principal
criticisms or difficulties. Yet when Burman sat down with
Descartes he had earmarked in advance over seventy texts
from the *Meditations, Replies to Objections, Notes against a
Programme, Principles,* and *Discourse*; and he proceeded to
raise over eighty specific points covering some of the most
vital issues in Cartesian philosophy. Here then we have no
journalistic interview but the most detailed and comprehensive philosophical discussion. If we combine this with
the fact that Descartes, usually so cautious and reticent, here
holds forth with remarkable openness, and add the fact that
the *Conversation,* held less than two years before his death,
represents, apart from correspondence, the last recorded
expression of Descartes' philosophical views, then the
importance and fascination of this remarkable work need
no further explaining.

BACKGROUND TO THE MEETING

Nothing is known of the encounter between Descartes and Burman beyond the bare bones that can be gleaned from the manuscript. On the first page there is a brief title—'Responsiones Renati des Cartes ad quasdam difficultates ex Meditationibus ejus etc. ab ipso haustae'—and then the place and date: 'Egmondae, April. 16. 1648'. Alongside, in the margin, we find (in the same hand) 'Per Burmannum qui 20 Aprilis communicavit Amstelodami cum Claubergio, ex cujus MSto ipsemet descripsi. Dordraci. Ad 13 et 14 Julii.' And at the very end of the MS. are the words 'Amstelodami, April. 20 anno 1648'.

It seems, then, that Burman came to Descartes' country retreat at Egmond on 16 April 1648. The two men appear to have dined together (during the Conversation, Descartes illustrates the point that one can have two thoughts at once by saying 'I now have the thought that I am talking and that I am eating' [see text, piece No. 6]). During and after the meal, Burman went through the passages he had prepared from Descartes' works (he evidently brought his texts with him) and put his questions to the philosopher. The two conversed in Latin as was still perfectly natural and normal in the seventeenth century for two scholars from different countries. In any case, Descartes' Dutch and Burman's French were probably both too shaky to make either vernacular language a really comfortable medium for discussion. We know that Descartes, despite his long residence in Holland, never fully mastered the Dutch tongue (cf. AT xii. 275). But he was, of course, a fluent writer of Latin; and, as for speaking, the formal debates and dissertations which were part of the curriculum at La Flèche would have given him a lifelong proficiency.

The house at which Descartes received Burman was at Egmond Binnen, near Alkmaar. It is the countryside around Egmond which, if anywhere, deserves to be called Descartes' 'home': notorious for his frequent changes of residence in the 1620s and 1630s, he was a permanent resident here (apart from three visits to France) from May 1643 until he left for Sweden in August 1649; his first house was at Egmond op den Hoef; then from 1644 onwards he lived at near-by Egmond Binnen. Here he was able to enjoy the quiet and secluded existence which he so valued—keeping to a simple routine and maintaining a careful diet based largely on produce from his kitchen garden (AT xii. 127–8; iv. 640).

At the time of Burman's visit, Descartes, then fifty-two years old, was famous throughout Europe. With the exception of the *Passions of the Soul* (written earlier, but not published till 1649), all the works to be published in his lifetime had appeared, culminating with his *magnum opus*, the *Principles*, in 1644. Frans Burman, by contrast, was at the start of his career—a young man of twenty. (Later, in 1664, he was to become Professor of Theology at the University of Utrecht; his two-volume *Synopsis Theologiae* appeared in 1671; he died in 1679.) Born in Leyden in 1628, Burman was the son of a Protestant minister who had fled to Leyden from Frankenthal during the Palatinate wars. How the young Burman gained an introduction to Descartes is not known: it is possible that Descartes had met the Burman family at Leyden. (Adam points out that Abraham van der Heyden, Professor of Theology at Leyden, and later to become Burman's father-in-law, was a friend of Descartes. [AT xii. 483]) At all events, Descartes' young guest seems to have had a generous reception; the Conversation must have taken a considerable time, and apparently Burman was able to get through all the questions he had prepared without being cut short. That Descartes was so free with his time should not be too much of a surprise; though he preferred the solitude of Egmond to the strains of Paris or the Dutch university towns, he was not the complete recluse which he is sometimes painted during this period. We know, for example, that his friend the Abbé Picot stayed with him at Egmond for three months, and that the philosopher was capable of taking a keen interest in local affairs (AT xii. 475, 482). And no doubt Descartes found a lively discussion with a keen and quickwitted student more congenial than the theological debates with the 'learned doctors' at which he so often struggled to defend the orthodoxy of his views.

Four days after the Conversation, so our marginal note in the MS. tells us, Burman made contact with Clauberg at

Amsterdam. Here, apparently, the final version of the *Conversation*, as we now have it, was completed: as noted above, the words 'Amstelodami, April. 20 anno 1648' appear at the very end of our MS.; moreover, the unknown scribe who produced our MS. at 'Dordracum' (Dordrecht) on 13 and 14 July states that he copied Clauberg's manuscript ('ex cujus MSto ipsemet descripsi'). It is impossible to say how much Clauberg contributed to the final version; possibly he helped Burman to write up his notes of the meeting; but it seems more likely (see section on authenticity below, p. xvi) that Burman already had a full and comprehensive account of the discussion which Clauberg merely copied. The man to whom we owe the survival of the *Conversation* was later to become a fairly well known exponent of the Cartesian school, though at the time of the meeting at Amsterdam he was only twenty-six—six years older than Burman. Born in 1622, John Clauberg became Professor of Philosophy and Theology first at Herborn and then at Duisburg (1651). His *Defensio Cartesiana* appeared in 1652, and in 1658 he published a detailed commentary on the *Meditations* (*Paraphrasis in Renati Des Cartes Meditationes*). This last work makes use in various places of material from the *Conversation* (see, for example, Commentary below, p. 54). Clauberg's collected works were published posthumously at Amsterdam in 1691.

THE MANUSCRIPT; EDITIONS

Clauberg's manuscript was copied by the unknown scribe of Dordrecht into a small quarto notebook. This later found its way into the library of the German theologian Crusius[1] (1715–75) (a note on the first page reads: 'Ex. Bibl. M. Crusii', with the date 1751); and it now reposes in the Niedersächsische Staats- und Universitätsbibliothek at Göttingen (MS. Philol. 264).

The handwriting and lay-out of the MS. leave much to be desired. The copyist's script is messy, and often—especially near the end—nearly illegible; the formation of the letters is not consistent, and there are frequent indecipherable

---

[1] A clue to the appearance of our MS. here lies in the fact that the Crusius family were connected by marriage to Burman's in-laws, the Van der Heydens. Cf. THIJSSEN-SCHOUTE, p. 668.

abbreviations which have to be interpreted according to context. Except for the first page, where underlining is used, there is nothing to distinguish the introductory quotations from the text, and often only a page-number at the beginning of a line will indicate that a new passage for discussion has been introduced. In deciphering the copyist's writing I have been greatly indebted to Adam, who has produced a clear and well laid out Latin text in Volume Five of his standard edition of Descartes (AT v. 146–79). The only criticism one can make of Adam as an editor is that he sometimes seems to have been over-zealous in emending the original where good sense can be made of it as it stands; the places where I have departed from Adam's text enough to affect the translation are indicated in the Commentary.

The *Conversation* was first published by the *Revue bourguignonne de l'Enseignement supérieur* in 1896. Apart from the standard text in Adam and Tannery already referred to, Adam published a text and French translation of the *Conversation*, with short notes,[1] in 1937, under the title *Entretien avec Burman*. (Although this title has no counterpart in the original Latin manuscript it has become the label under which the *Conversation* is most widely known.) This edition contains one or two minor corrections and improvements on the earlier text. There is another French version of the *Conversation*, by André Bridoux, in the Pléiade edition of Descartes (1953).

FORMAT AND PRESENTATION

The Latin original is divided into eighty-two small pieces, which I have numbered for convenience. The number, in square brackets, appears before each piece. I have referred to the pieces in the Commentary and elsewhere by the appropriate number with the prefix 'CB'—for 'Conversation with Burman'—for example 'CB 25'. Each piece in the text comprises (A) a quotation from one of the published works of Descartes and (B) some sort of discussion or commentary. (The only exception to this is CB 48, which

---

[1] These notes (eight short pages) are exceedingly brief and contain almost no exegesis of the text or philosophical criticism; though they do include one or two helpful cross-references to Descartes' writings which I have made use of in the Commentary.

contains some general remarks not related to a specific text.)

(A) Burman took all his quotations from the Latin editions of Descartes' works published in the 1640s by the house of Elzevir of Amsterdam. He introduced and identified each quotation by a reference, as follows:

(i) quotations from the *Meditations* and the *Replies to Objections* (CB 1–47): by page-numbers of the 1642 edition. (This was the second edition of the *Meditations*—the first was published in Paris in 1641—but it is generally regarded as the definitive edition (cf. AT xii. xi ff.) and was the first to contain all seven sets of *Objections* and *Replies*.)

(ii) quotation from the *Notes against a Programme* (CB 49): by page-number of the first edition of 1648.

(iii) quotations from the *Principles of Philosophy* (CB 50–75): by Book and Article numbers of the first edition of 1644.

(iv) quotations from the *Discourse on Method* (CB 76–82): by page-numbers of the first edition of the Latin translation of the *Discourse*; this translation of the original French edition of 1637 was made by Descartes' friend Étienne de Courcelles and published in 1644; it was seen and approved by the author.

In my text, I have retained Burman's original references at the beginning of each quotation (these may still be used, since Adam and Tannery indicate the original Elzevir pagination in their presentation of the texts in question); but I have also inserted—in brackets at the end of each quotation—volume and page references to the Adam and Tannery edition and to the standard English translation of Descartes by Haldane and Ross. Nineteen of the pieces from the *Principles* are not translated in Haldane and Ross; of these, six are translated in Anscombe and Geach's selection of Descartes' writings, and in these cases I have referred to the page-number of the Anscombe and Geach volume.

The quotations in the original MS. are very brief: in each case Burman reproduces only the few Latin words relevant to the precise point he wishes to raise. It seemed to me desirable to indicate a little more of the context in each case, rather than forcing the reader constantly to turn up the original passage in Descartes. Accordingly, I have supplied rather fuller quotations than Burman provides. My procedure has been to go back to the original Latin text from which the words quoted by Burman are taken, and translate as much of the relevant passage as seemed necessary to make the context reasonably clear. The words in my translation which correspond to the few key words actually quoted by Burman have been italicized.

(B) The commentary or discussion which follows each quotation takes two main forms, viz. (i) straight commentary and (ii) dialogue with objections and replies. (i) The former can vary from a few brief words glossing a phrase or clarifying a point in the text (e.g. CB 8, 40) to a more extended piece of continuous prose (CB 21, 57). These pieces of commentary are presented as recording the direct pronouncements of Descartes, or 'the author' (*auctor*) as he is called throughout. The grammatical form of the Latin is a curious mixture. Sometimes oratio recta is used (CB 25, 30), and Descartes may refer to himself in the first person (CB 29); sometimes there is the indirect construction ('the author says/holds that . . .' etc.) (CB 2, 3, 80); sometimes there is a mixture of both constructions (e.g. CB 58, which starts in oratio obliqua and slips into oratio recta). (ii) The second, and more frequent, form is that of a dialogue, in which Burman raises some objection, generally quite briefly, and Descartes replies, often at considerable length; sometimes there will be a further objection and a further reply, and so on (CB 9). The replies of Descartes exhibit the same characteristic mixture of direct and indirect speech already described. The letter R is generally used in the MS. to designate these replies of Descartes, and I have followed this device in the translation. (Where an R is placed in brackets, it is omitted in the original.) I have also followed the practice of Adam in marking with an O, in brackets thus [O], the objections and questions attributable to Burman (in the MS., R is the only mark provided). Passages without any letter prefix are the pieces of straight commentary described under (i) above. Finally, it should be noted that the straight commentary form sometimes breaks into the dialogue form in the course of a single piece (CB 22, 50). There is a potential editorial difficulty when this happens, since there is nothing in the MS. to show where a comment of Descartes ends and an objection of Burman's begins. In fact there is generally no great problem about how a passage is to be split up between the two speakers; but once or twice (e.g. CB 28) I have quarrelled with Adam's distribution of the lines.

AUTHENTICITY AND RELIABILITY AS A SOURCE

No one, so far as I know, has ever questioned the authenticity of the *Conversation*, and there is no reason to doubt that it is the record of a genuine meeting. But it is important to remember that the text we have is not the work of Descartes but of Burman (perhaps with Clauberg's assistance); as a source, the piece thus lacks the direct authority of Descartes' published works, or even his letters. It is true that Descartes' replies to Burman are described in the MS. as 'obtained directly from the man himself' (*ab ipso haustae*): Burman was proud of having got his material 'straight from the horse's mouth'. But we still have to face the question of how accurate a reporter Burman was. Did he meticulously record Descartes' comments, or do his own, possibly mistaken, impressions and interpretations creep in? Then again, we must face the possibility that Burman made only the briefest of notes while talking to Descartes, and waited until his meeting with Clauberg, four days later, before writing up a full version. The worst possibility of all is that the version that has come down to us is not the work of the actual interviewer at all, but the imaginative reconstruction of Clauberg, prompted by Burman's verbal account of the meeting.

Here I think that the style of the MS. can help us. It seems to me that the jumbled and bizarre mixture of direct and indirect speech (described above) argues strongly for the authenticity of the record. If the *Conversation* had been freely written up four days after it occurred, we should expect a much more fluent and grammatically uniform style. What we in fact have is just what one would expect from someone hurriedly taking down remarks as they were being spoken: if one looks at the notes most people take at a lecture or discussion, I suggest that one will be likely to find just such a mixture of oratio recta and oratio obliqua as we find in the *Conversation*; the note-taker will slip back and forth from the actual words of the lecturer, to the indirect construction ('*X*'s view is that . . .').

This argument is not of course conclusive, but I think it should incline us to regard the *Conversation* as a transcript of—or at least closely based on—the notes taken down directly by Burman at the time of the interview. In fact, even a full verbatim account of the proceedings is quite within the bounds of possibility, given that Burman employed the usual mixture of abbreviations and private shorthand which all of us develop. This sounds optimistic until one remembers the special nature of the *Conversation*. The discussion is not free-floating, but is broken into eighty-two short pieces, each closely tied to the particular text which Burman had earmarked in advance. So there would have been plenty of pauses, plenty of chances for Burman to get his account up to date before moving on to the next passage which he wished to draw to Descartes' attention.

Even if Burman did take down Descartes' comments word for word, this does not entail that he was infallible. The best reporters make mistakes—a remark misheard, a wrong emphasis.[1] But I think there are grounds for supposing that Burman's reporting was, on the whole, very faithful. Over and over again, in the remarks attributed to Descartes, the language and phrasing exhibit the characteristic ring and authority of the philosopher (see, for example, the firm replies at CB 49 and CB 7; or the fluent analysis at CB 79). Such stylistic criteria are, notoriously, dependent on subjective impressions; but we have the more objective criterion of content as a further check. We are not in the position of having to reconstruct a Socratic Descartes from the account of a Platonic Burman: Descartes' own prolific writings elsewhere, in the published works and the correspondence, can be used as a touchstone for testing the plausibility of the remarks which Burman puts into his mouth. This test should not be applied too rigidly: if the *Conversation* did nothing but repeat exactly what Descartes says elsewhere, it would not be of great philosophical

[1] Adam suggests one particular area in which Burman may have gone astray: 'le jeune huguenot Burman, à qui Descartes vu de loin apparaissait comme un papiste, exagéra sans doute . . . l'indifférence et l'irrévérence même de ses propos touchant les vérités morales et religieuses' (AT xii. 484). But Descartes' reported comments on ethics and religion seem to me quite in character: see commentary on CB 80, 58, 78.

interest; and in fact there is much that Descartes says to Burman which is either new, or formulated in a strikingly new way. But always, so far as I can see, the new material meshes with the fundamental structure of Descartes' philosophy; nothing is said which vitiates the coherence and consistency of the Cartesian system (or rather, where there are inconsistencies, they are ones which are already endemic in the system in any case). This is not to say that there are no difficulties; as with any interesting philosophical work there are puzzles and problem passages—some of these are discussed below, and in the Commentary. But it seems to me that there is nothing attributed to Descartes which is so bizarre or implausible as to convict Burman of substantial carelessness or inaccuracy.

VALUE AND PHILOSOPHICAL IMPORTANCE

I began by noticing two of the features which give the *Conversation* its special appeal—the unique directness and vividness of the interview format, and the range and depth of the discussion. For both these virtues, a great deal of the credit must go to the young Burman.

First, in conducting his interview Burman is no passive disciple drinking in the master's pronouncements. His questions are searching and critical; and when he is not satisfied with a reply he will not let matters rest, but will return for a second attack (cf. CB 6, 23, 24). It is this which gives us such a sense of immediacy—of confrontation, and which makes the *Conversation* so much more vital and readable than the more formal wrangling of the *Objections and Replies* or the more static explanatory passages in the letters.

Secondly, Burman understood the value of careful research and preparation. By earmarking in advance over seventy key passages from Descartes' works, Burman made sure that the interview would not be vague and general, but would tackle specific issues in depth. Moreover, despite its wide range, there is sufficient detail in the *Conversation* to cast a fresh light on many of the most crucial problems of Descartes' philosophy; as Adam enthusiastically notes, 'toutes les grandes questions de la philosophie de Descartes, toutes les difficultés qu'elle soulève, y sont examinées'.[1] A

[1] ADAM, p. xii.

glance at the Conspectus on pp. 121 ff. will show that this is no exaggeration: the 'big questions' discussed include the malignant demon, the Cogito, and the Cartesian Circle; the nature of thought and the theory of mental substance; adequate knowledge, essences, and the innateness doctrine; and Descartes' theory of the will. Particularly interesting is the discussion of the activities of the mind: the 'hybrid' concepts of imagination and sense-perception, and the important distinction between imagination, 'conception', and understanding.

A welcome feature of the *Conversation* from the point of view of the modern reader—though in some ways a surprising one—is that so much material is devoted to enduring philosophical issues, while comparatively little is concerned with the niceties of seventeenth-century theology. Burman, the son of a minister, and himself later to become a professional theologian, would perhaps have welcomed spending more time on matters relating to the Christian faith; but time and again Descartes steers him away from this area with the slogan 'let us leave that for the theologians to explain' (CB 32, 58, 82). Another reason why the discussion does not get bogged down with theological technicalities is that Burman, a Protestant, is less interested in cross-questioning Descartes on the finer points of Catholic dogma which occupy so much time in some of the *Objections and Replies* and the correspondence.

The result is that the great bulk of the *Conversation* centres around aspects of Cartesian philosophy that are of living interest to philosophers today—the key issues in Theory of Knowledge, Philosophy of Mind, and Philosophical Psychology on which Descartes' thought is so fertile. Even in the passages which deal with the last three books of the *Principles* (CB 53–75) there is something of a philosophical bias: admittedly the discussion of points arising out of some of Descartes' more bizarre scientific theories will nowadays probably interest only the historian of science; but there remains enough material to provide some fascinating insights into Descartes' views on the philosophy and methodology of science.

Overall, then, the *Conversation* is a rich and absorbing work, a tribute to the intelligence of the Dutchman who engineered it, and a fresh and valuable illumination of the genius of Descartes at the height of his powers and maturity.

II
SOME CRUCIAL TOPICS

I shall now discuss briefly four of the most important contributions of the *Conversation* to our understanding of Cartesian philosophy.

(i) *The Cogito*

Perhaps the most debated question about the proposition 'I exist', the first foothold in the Cartesian assault on scepticism, is whether we are supposed to know it immediately and directly, or only mediately, via some process of reasoning. Does Descartes mean us to infer or deduce our existence by means of an argument (as the *ergo* in 'cogito ergo sum' would suggest); or are we supposed to arrive at knowledge of our existence by means of a simple act of intuition? The question raised in the *Conversation* is a different, but closely related one, viz. that of whether the Cogito involves a syllogism. In a famous passage in the Second Replies, Descartes seems quite adamant:

When we take note of the fact that we are thinking things, this is a primary notion, which is not derived from any syllogism. For when someone says 'I think, therefore I am, or I exist', he does not deduce existence from thought by means of a syllogism, but recognizes it as a simple intuition of the mind, as if it were a thing known *per se*. This is clear from the fact that, if he were deducing it by means of a syllogism, he would have to have known previously the major 'everything which thinks is, or exists' (*illud omne quod cogitat est sive existit*); yet in fact of course he learns it instead from experiencing in his own case that it is impossible that he should think without existing. (AT vii. 140; HR ii. 38)

The man who arrives at 'cogito ergo sum' (let us call him the 'cogitator' for short) does not require prior knowledge of the major premiss

(1) Everything which thinks exists.

There is an important discussion about this passage at CB 4. But before one can deal with the substance of Descartes' comments, a textual difficulty must be faced. Challenging Descartes about the assertion in the Second Replies that the cogitator does not deduce existence from thought by means of a syllogism, Burman asks: 'is not the opposite asserted at *Principles* I, 10?' (line 1). Descartes apparently agrees, and goes on to explain why he 'said in the *Principles* that the major premiss comes first' (line 5). Something seems to have gone wrong here, for if we examine the relevant part of the *Principles*, we find that neither syllogisms nor major premisses are anywhere mentioned in the discussion of the Cogito.

At first sight this appears to present a difficult dilemma. To accept the text as a correct record of what was said, would seem to entail that Descartes was less than particular about the accuracy of quotations from his published work; to reject the text would mean that Burman misreported one of the most vital exchanges in the *Conversation*, in which case the general reliability of the *Conversation* as a source would be called into question.

In fact, though, the misquotation is not totally damning. For although Descartes does not talk of syllogisms and major premisses in *Principles* I, 10, he does say the following:

When I said that this proposition, '*I think, therefore I am*', was of all propositions the first and most certain which anyone who philosophizes in an orderly way comes up against, I did not by saying that deny that one must first know *what knowledge is, what existence and certainty are,* and *that it is impossible that that which thinks should not exist (fieri non posse ut id quod cogitet non existat)*, and so forth; but, because these are very simple notions and ones which on their own do not furnish us with knowledge of any existing thing, I did not think them worth listing [AT viii. 8].

So the *Principles do* assert that the cogitator needs knowledge of the general principle

(2) It is impossible to think without existing.

However, we are still far from out of the wood. For the *Principles* text describes proposition (2) as one of the 'very simple notions which on their own do not furnish us with knowledge of any existing thing' ('. . . nullius rei existentis notitiam prabent'). Yet under the rules of traditional Aristotelian logic, a universal affirmative proposition like (1) was regarded as having existential import (i.e. as entailing that some thinking thing exists). Would not Descartes have been keenly aware of this, and so made a sharp distinction between (2), the 'notion' in the *Principles* lacking existential import, and (1), the 'major' which Burman makes him substitute for it at CB 4? What is more, it is sometimes suggested that Descartes' denial that the Cogito involves a syllogism (in the Second Replies) was made precisely to avoid the danger of a *petitio principii* that would arise if 'cogito ergo sum' were derived from a major premiss with existential import. If this view is correct, then the very last thing Descartes would have done is to go along with a careless assimilation of (2) to (1).

I am inclined to think, however, that when Descartes discussed the proposition 'everything which thinks exists' the difficulty that this might be construed as entailing a singular existential proposition simply did not occur to him. This may seem a tall order. But, firstly, the existential import of universal affirmatives, though it is a feature of the Aristotelian system, is not a glaring feature (its rejection would leave the validity of many of the most common argument patterns quite untouched[1]). There is a danger here of projecting back the mental habits of the twentieth century on to the seventeenth: the logical status of universal affirmatives and the difficulties of the Aristotelian square of opposition have bulked large in the minds of philosophers only since the advent of alternative logical systems. Secondly, at no point when Descartes discusses the syllogism does he show any awareness of the dangers of a *petitio principii* (nor is this raised by any of the objectors). When discussing the issue with Clerselier, Descartes makes it clear that he regards the supposed involvement of a major premiss in the Cogito as dangerous only because it lays him open to the charge of having been careless in his method of doubt and allowed an unexamined prejudice into his reasoning (AT ix. 206; HR ii. 127).

In view of this, I think it is quite possible that Descartes was capable of assimilating (1) and (2). I do not mean that if challenged he would have maintained that there was no difference whatever between the two formulations. But I suggest that he might well have maintained that 'Omne id quod cogitat est sive existit' and 'fieri non potest ut id quod

---

[1] In the first figure, for example, all four principal moods (Barbara, Celarent, Darii, Ferio) remain untouched; only the 'weakened' moods (AAI, EAO) are affected by the question of existential import.

cogitet non existat' were both ways of referring to the general principle involved in the inference 'cogito ergo sum'. If this is right, there is no sound reason for supposing that Burman got his notes into a muddle at this point, or that his reconstruction of the argument is less than substantially accurate.

We may now turn to the substance of Descartes' reply to Burman over the Cogito. Whatever the textual problems at CB 4, there is a general difficulty confronting Descartes which Burman has succeeded in drawing attention to. Put at its simplest, the question is: does the cogitator, or does he not, require prior knowledge of a general principle connecting thought with existence? And why do the *Principles* and *Replies* appear to give conflicting answers on this?

To prepare the way for Descartes' solution, it is important to notice a very close parallel in the language of the apparently clashing passages. Although the Second Replies text denies that the major (1) is used as a premiss for deduction, it does assert (see the last two lines of the passage quoted above) that the cogitator *learns* this premiss (ipsam [majorem] . . . discit) from what he experiences in his own case. What he experiences in his own case is a particular proposition, namely (to put it in oratio recta),

(3) It is impossible that I should think without existing.

It will be seen at once that this bears a close formal similarity to the general proposition (2) which the cogitator is said to require knowledge of in the *Principles*. The resemblance is even more striking in the Latin texts. The original of (2), 'fieri non potest ut id quod cogitet non existat' (AT viii. 8), closely corresponds to the wording of (3) in the Second Replies: '. . . fieri non posse ut cogitet nisi existat' (AT vii. 140). (Unfortunately, most English versions of the passage in the *Principles* follow Picot's French version, which has the rather compressed 'pour penser il faut être' for the sentence in question; and the parallelism has therefore gone unnoticed.)

The explanation of what is going on here, and the key to the correct interpretation of the Cogito, depend, I suggest, on some vital observations Descartes has to make about the way in which we normally possess knowledge of certain general propositions; and it is here that the contribution of the *Conversation* is invaluable. The general proposition 'whatever thinks exists' is called a 'general notion' (*notio generalis*) at CB 4, line 11;[1] as already noted (above p. xxi), a similar expression, 'very simple notion' (*notio simplicissima*) is used in the *Principles* (AT viii. 8) to describe our proposition (2). Now 'notion' seems to be something of a technical term for Descartes. It is invariably used to describe basic logical truths—'common principles and axioms' as they are called at CB 1, line 13. Here is what Descartes says about these principles at CB 1: 'since [these principles] are present in us from birth with such clarity, and since we experience them inside ourselves, we neglect them and think about them only in a confused manner, *but never in the abstract, or apart from material things and particular instances*' (lines 17 ff.; my italics). Descartes makes the point again at CB 4, this time in connection with the Cogito: 'As I have explained before, we do not separate out these general propositions from the particular instances; rather, *it is in the particular instances that we think of them*' (lines 12 ff.; my italics). This is sound enough as a matter of empirical psychology. A child, for example, will be able to reject a particular contradiction as false, without being able expressly to formulate the 'general notion' that every proposition of the form '$P \;\&\; \sim P$' must be false.[2] In such a case, we may say with Descartes that the knowledge of the general principle has not been 'separated out' from the particular instance.

It is clear from all this that Descartes is aware of a crucial ambiguity in saying that someone *knows*, for example, the principle of non-contradiction: does the knowledge have to be explicit (i.e. does the knower have to be able to formulate the principle explicitly), or is it sufficient for him to be able to recognize its truth in 'particular instances'? (This is part

---

[1] Interestingly, Descartes uses the same phrase when discussing the major premiss (1) with Clerselier (loc. cit.)—a point which further supports the case argued above for the reliability of Burman's reporting on this issue.

[2] Cf. Descartes' own comment to Clerselier: 'Quand on enseigne à un enfant les éléments de la Géometrie, on ne lui fera point entendre en général que . . . *le tout est plus grand que ses parties*, si on ne lui en montre des exemples en des cas particuliers.' (loc. cit.)

of a general difficulty in the use of the verb 'to know': compare 'he knows the principles of English grammar'). If we now relate this to the Cogito, the precise content of the claim that prior knowledge of a general principle is necessary for the cogitator will hinge on whether the knowledge is supposed to be explicit or implicit. And Descartes' position on this comes out at CB 4. Prior knowledge of a general principle is, it seems, involved (line 1); 'but it does not follow that I am always expressly and explicitly aware of its priority' (line 7/8). And Descartes goes on to make the point quoted above that one may know a general principle only in a particular instance.

In the light of this, the *Principles* can be reconciled with the Second Replies. It is true in a sense that the cogitator needs prior knowledge of the general principle (2) asserting the impossibility of thought without existence (*Principles*). But the knowledge need not be explicit (cf. CB 4). The individual has the general principle implanted in him from birth, but he is not explicitly aware of it (CB 1). He recognizes it only in the singular, particular case (3), by seeing in his own case that it is impossible that he should think without existing (Second Replies). And it is this recognition, coupled with the indubitable awareness of the fact that he is thinking, that enables him to know the proposition 'sum' with certainty.

What, then, of the question we originally started with, viz. whether the knowledge of one's existence is, for Descartes, immediate or derived? In the light of what has emerged it is easy to see that the question is really a misleading one, since the alternatives are not mutually exclusive. The knowledge of one's existence is derivative in the sense that it implicitly depends on a general logical principle (or 'notion') asserting the impossibility of thought without existence. But it is immediate in the sense that the cogitator need not be aware of this principle except in its particular application to himself; so that the knowledge of his existence may come upon him not as a deduction from a general premiss, but 'as if it were a thing known *per se*'.[1]

---

[1] Second Replies, quoted above, p. xx. A lot of recent discussion has centred on the precise interpretation of the phrase 'tanquam rem per se notam'; for some of the difficulties see KENNY (1), p. 54.

(ii) *Knowledge and the Circle*

Lastly, as to the fact that I was not guilty of circularity (*circulum non commiserim*) when I said that the only reason we have for being sure that what we clearly and distinctly perceive is true is the fact that God exists; but that we are sure God exists only because we perceive this clearly: I have already given an adequate explanation of this point in the reply to the Second Objections, Nos. 3 and 4, where I made a distinction between what we in fact perceive clearly and what we remember having perceived clearly. (Descartes' reply to Arnauld: AT vii. 245; HR ii. 114)

It seems there is a circle. For in the Third Meditation the author uses axioms to prove the existence of God, even though he is not yet certain of not being deceived about these. (CB 6, lines 1–4)

Descartes' procedure in the *Meditations* does not seem to involve a *petitio principii* in the ordinary sense; the author does not attempt to rig an argument by slipping into the premisses the proposition he is setting out to prove. What worried Arnauld and Burman is what might be called an epistemological circularity: a violation, not of the formal rules of deductive logic, but of the careful methodological procedure which Descartes claims to follow in his reconstruction of human knowledge. This procedure is stated explicitly in the Second Replies, where Descartes says that in the *Meditations* he tried to adhere most strictly (*accuratissime*) to a particular order: 'The order consists simply in the fact that the propositions put forward first have to be known *without any help from those that follow*, and then that the remainder should be arranged in such a way that their demonstration depends solely on what has gone before' (AT vii. 155; HR ii. 48 [italics mine]. See also the *Search After Truth*: AT x. 526–7; HR i. 327). It is a violation of this rule that Burman in effect alleges. How are we supposed to know the axioms required to prove God's existence? The author is 'not yet certain of not being deceived about these'; and thus the whole carefully planned structure of the build-up of knowledge appears threatened.

Now Descartes clearly supposed that he had an adequate reply to this worrying charge. But until he spoke to Burman he had explained his response in remarkably obscure language—so much so that many modern commentators have, I believe, completely misunderstood his meaning. Let us look first at the earlier formulations of his defence.

(a) *The reply to Arnauld*

Here Descartes seems to rest all the weight on a distinction between what is *in fact* clearly and distinctly perceived and what we merely *remember* having clearly and distinctly perceived. Why on earth should Descartes bring in memory at this point? One popular modern view on this is that he is correcting a misapprehension about the role of God in his system: what he is saying, on this view, is that God's role is not that of guarantor of clearly and distinctly perceived truths (despite any impression to the contrary that the Fifth Meditation may have given), but merely the guarantor of the veracity of memory (see DONEY (2), pp. 326 ff.). According to this view, when I clearly and distinctly perceive P, I can know the truth of P even if I do not yet know that there is a God; after I have proved God's existence, however, I can know the truth of P even if I merely 'remember' that I once clearly and distinctly perceived it.[1]

But notice what a very odd claim Descartes would be making, if he meant to assert this; he would be flying in the face of the universal acknowledgement of the fallibility of memory. (The fact that the remembering involved here relates to a special sort of proposition, viz. 'that I clearly and distinctly perceived P', makes no difference to this point. If I can 'remember' having had a cup of coffee this morning, when in fact I did not, there seems no reason why I cannot equally 'remember' having clearly and distinctly perceived the truth of Euclid's thirteenth theorem this morning, when in fact I did not.) But not only *would* it have been very odd if Descartes had advanced a thesis like this, but there is very strong evidence in the *Conversation* that he did not in fact do so. At CB 5, where Descartes and Burman discuss the question of the reliability of the human mind, and whether God can deceive, Burman makes the point that, even after God's existence has been proved and I know that my mind does not deceive me (*non fallit ingenium*), yet still my memory may deceive me (*fallit memoria*), since I may

[1] By putting the word 'remember' in inverted commas, I merely mean to mark the obvious fact that the verb is to be taken in what is sometimes called the 'weak sense'—i.e. the sense which leaves it open whether a memory experience is veridical. This is opposed to the 'strong sense' of the verb, where 'I remember that P' entails P. Of course, it does not need God, or anyone else, to guarantee the veracity of memory in this strong sense.

think I remember something which I do not in fact remember. This is because memory is weak (*imbecillis*) (lines 14–19). Descartes, and this is the vital point, implicitly accepts this. He says that he has nothing to say on the subject of memory: 'everyone should test himself to see whether he is good at remembering. If he has any doubts he should make use of written notes and so forth to help him' (lines 20–23). Here Descartes is clearly taking up a cautious, common sense position *vis-à-vis* the possibility of my mistakenly thinking I remember having clearly and distinctly perceived Euclid's thirteenth theorem this morning. He sensibly tells us to check our memory by means of the usual aids. This is not the suggestion of a man who regards the veracity of memory as guaranteed (or even made more likely) once God's existence has been established.

(b) *The reply to the Second Objections*

The authors of the Second Objections had cited as a focus for their accusation an awkward passage in the Fifth Meditation; they complained: 'according to your statement, you cannot be certain of anything, or know anything clearly and distinctly unless you first know certainly and clearly that God exists' (AT vii. 125–5; HR ii. 26). Descartes did not, in fact, make this statement in exactly these words. But what he does say in the Fifth Meditation apparently comes down to the same thing: 'the certainty of everything else depends on this very thing [knowledge of God's existence], so that apart from this nothing can ever be perfectly known' (AT vii. 69, lines 13–15; HR i. 183; cf. *Principles* I, 30). And later on we are told that it is from the knowledge that God exists and is not a deceiver that 'I have gathered that whatever I clearly and distinctly perceive is, necessarily, true' (collegi omnia, quae clare et distincte percipio, necessario esse vera; AT vii. 70). Both these quotations ring out like warning bells to those on the look-out for a circle.

What happens, however, in the Second Replies, is that Descartes puts a vital qualification on his statement in the *Meditations* that all knowledge depends on God: 'When I said that we can know nothing for certain until we know that God exists, I expressly declared that I was speaking merely of knowledge of those conclusions which can be recalled when we are no longer attending to the reasoning which led us to their deduction' (AT vii. 140; HR ii. 38). The crucial concept introduced here is that of *attention*. (It is true that 'recalling' is also mentioned, but the reference to memory, though there is, as we shall see, a perfectly good reason for it, is in a sense a red herring.) The distinction Descartes is getting at is that between our knowledge of clearly and distinctly perceived propositions *at the time when we are attending to them*, and our knowledge of such propositions when we are not attending to them. The former type of knowledge is an exception to the rule that 'all knowledge depends on God'.

(c) *The reply to Burman*

What I have just said would be only a tentative interpretation of what is, after all, a rather cryptic sentence, were it not for the valuable evidence of the *Conversation*. For at CB 6, we have the most explicit and clear statement of Descartes' reply to the charge of circularity. Talking of the axioms used to prove the existence of God Descartes says: 'I know that I am not deceived with regard to them, *because I am actually paying* attention to them; and *for as long as I do pay attention to them* I am certain that I am not being deceived.'[1] In this idea of the mind's focusing on, or attending to, a proposition we have the key to Descartes' attempt to break the circle. At the time when we are actually focusing on a proposition, then, if we clearly and distinctly perceive it to be true, we cannot be mistaken—we *know* we are not being deceived.[2]

The importance which Descartes attaches to this concept of mental attention emerges elsewhere in the *Conversation*.

---

[1] Italics mine. The oratio obliqua of the original Latin is reproduced in my translation of CB 6, lines 5–9, q.v. The Latin reads: 'scit se in iis non falli quoniam ad ea attendit, quamdiu a[utem] id facit, certus est se non falli.'

[2] The reliability of the *Conversation* on this issue is confirmed by Descartes' reply to Bourdin, who had asked how the attainment of knowledge was possible in Descartes' system, given the extent of Cartesian doubt. Descartes points out that when he said 'there was nothing which we may not doubt', this was 'in the First Meditation, where I was supposing that I was not attending to anything which I clearly perceived' (in Prima Meditatione in qua supponebam me non attendere ad quicquam quod clare perciperem) (Seventh Replies: AT vii. 460; HR ii. 266).

Right at the beginning, Descartes says that the common principles and axioms (like 'it is impossible that the same thing should both be and not be') cannot be denied by anyone who *carefully focuses his attention on them* (attente ad illa animadvertit; CB 1, line 26). And at CB 81 Descartes uses the same idea, when summing up his position on the circle. If we did not know that God was the source of truth, then however clear our ideas were we should not know they were true, says Descartes, restating what he had said in the Fifth Meditation. But then he adds: 'I mean of course when we were not *paying attention* to them (cum ad eas non adverteremus), and when we merely remembered that we had clearly and distinctly perceived them. For on other occasions, when we *do* pay attention to the truths themselves (quando ad ipsas veritates advertimus), even though we may not know God exists we cannot be in any doubt about them. Otherwise, we could not prove that God exists' (lines 3-9; my italics). These passages leave us in no doubt as to the thesis which Descartes wished to advance, and which he took to provide a defence against the charge of circularity. The thesis is that clearly and distinctly perceived propositions are, *while attended to*, epistemically self-guaranteeing.[1]

An objection to this interpretation is that it still leaves unclear the reasons for Descartes' harping on memory in

---

[1] Against this, a recent commentator has claimed: 'Descartes repeatedly asserts, without any qualification or limitation whatever, that as long as he is ignorant of God's existence he must fear that a proposition may be false even though he perceives it quite clearly and distinctly' (FRANKFURT, p. 166). This claim is based chiefly on Descartes' remark in the Third Meditation that some God may, if he wishes, cause me to go wrong 'even in those matters which I think I intuit with the utmost possible clarity with the eyes of the mind' (AT vii. 36, lines 10-12). But a crucial qualification follows in the very next sentence. When, says Descartes, he turns his attention to the *objects themselves* which he perceives clearly, he has to affirm that no deceiver could bring it about that 'I am nothing when I think I am something', or that 'two and three make more or less than five'. Frankfurt does acknowledge this passage, but he claims that Descartes only says that *he is persuaded* of the propositions in question while entertaining them—i.e. that he cannot doubt them, not that he knows they are true. But Descartes does assert that no deceiver could *bring it about* (efficere) that two plus three do not equal five; and this implies a claim about knowledge and truth, not just about psychological conviction. Compare the passage from CB 6 (quoted above) where Descartes says that because he is attending to the axioms he *knows* (scit) he is not being deceived.

his discussion of the circle. Although I have rejected the thesis that God is intended by Descartes to function as a guarantor of the veracity of memory, it must be admitted that the question of memory has an awkward habit of cropping up through the relevant parts of the *Meditations* and *Replies*. Even in the *Conversation*, Descartes seems to contrast focusing on P with remembering that P (CB 81; quoted above).

I think that the purpose of these references to memory is to highlight exactly what is meant by the crucial notion of attending, or focusing the mind. It is vital to notice that the self-guaranteeing nature of the propositions Descartes needs to break the circle cannot be regarded as something static or timeless. The guarantee is only operative, as it were, under very special conditions: it depends on, and is co-extensive with, the focusing of attention. If I am following the Cartesian programme, then I can indeed know the truth of the basic axioms while I attend to them. But as soon as I let my attention wander, even for a second, the 'guarantee' vanishes.

Now there is a severe limit to the number of propositions which the human mind can entertain at any one time. As Descartes remarks to Burman at CB 6, we can entertain more than *one* proposition at a time (lines 17 ff.) but the capacity of the mind is not infinite. The need for God in Descartes' theory of knowledge, and the sense in which all knowledge can be said to depend on him, now begins to emerge. For although we can have some knowledge without God (the knowledge of epistemically self-guaranteeing propositions), such knowledge would never, so to speak, *get* us anywhere. It would last only as long as the relevant proposition, or set of propositions, was actually being attended to. Thus, Descartes' constant reference to memory—to wondering whether, a moment ago, one clearly and distinctly perceived that P—is to emphasize the essential *disconnectedness* that would be a feature of knowledge without God. Suppose, however, that we attend to the axioms which prove God's existence—they are few enough, Descartes claims, for us to keep them all in focus at one time so that we can 'grasp the proof . . . in its entirety'.[1] Once we have arrived

[1] CB 6, *ad fin.* See, however, Commentary on CB 6, line 10.

at the proposition that God exists and is not a deceiver, then at last the possibility of developing a *systematic body* of knowledge becomes available.

But exactly *how* does knowledge of God's existence enable us to extend our knowledge beyond the flashes of self-guaranteeing intuition? One way to make the transition would be to show that God has given us a mind of infinite capacity for attention, or an infallible memory. But, as Descartes noted to Burman, this is not on—we have to make use of 'written notes and so forth' (CB 5, line 23). This is an interesting comment, because it shows the extent to which, for finite human beings, the development of knowledge is bound up with the use of aids and 'props'—*props which presuppose the existence of a stable external world*. Now the method of doubt in the First Meditation revealed how far the belief in such a world is ultimately a matter of faith. Once God's existence has been established, this basic prerequisite for the development of systematic knowledge can be reinstated. We can progress beyond the intuition of self-guaranteeing truths without being stopped short by the limitations of a finite mind.[1]

(iii) *Innate ideas*

The question, 'if some truths are innate, why do small children appear to be ignorant of them?', is a notoriously difficult one for innatists. (Compare Locke's strictures in the *Essay on Human Understanding*, Bk. I, Ch. 2, § 5.) The most common solution is that the ideas are present in embryonic form, waiting for a Socratic 'midwife' to draw them out (see Plato, *Theaetetus*, 149 ff.; *Meno*, 81 ff.). Thus, Leibniz speaks of innate ideas as 'des inclinations, des dispositions, des habitudes, ou des virtualités' (*Nouveaux Essais sur l'entendement humain*, Preface, para. 4). The difficulty with this solution is that the 'potential' or 'embryonic' presence of the ideas is such a vague concept that one wonders how it

---

[1] There is no space here to discuss whether the crucial notion of an 'epistemically self-guaranteeing proposition' is coherent. A defender of Descartes here would, I think, have to substantiate the claim that there are 'distinct' ideas (i.e. those whose content is *limited* to what is 'present and open to the attentive mind' (*Principles*, I, 45)). One would have to argue, e.g., that when I contemplate the meaning of '2 + 2 = 5', what is at present before my mind contains all that is necessary for the knowledge of the truth of this proposition. For this approach, cf. GEWIRTH.

really differs from the empiricist hypothesis that all ideas are gradually acquired through experience. '*S* has innate potential knowledge of *X*' risks becoming merely a portentous way of saying '*S* can learn *X*'.

Descartes himself had apparently toyed with this approach to the problem. In the *Notes against a Programme* he observes that the position of Regius (who had denied the need for postulating innate ideas) differs from his own only verbally. 'I never wrote or believed', he continues, 'that the mind needs ideas in the sense of something different from its faculty of thinking' (AT viiib. 357; HR i. 442). He goes on to say that ideas are innate in the sense in which certain diseases are innate: 'not that the infants of such families suffer from the diseases in their mother's womb, but because they are born with a certain disposition (*dispositio*) or liability (*facultas*) to contract them'.

In the *Conversation*, however (which took place less than a year after the writing of the *Notes*), Descartes seems to be trying to move away from the concept of potential or dispositional presence, by introducing an auxiliary hypothesis to account for the fact that the mind is not fully aware of the ideas in infancy. The ideas are present all right, Descartes apparently wants to say at CB 9, but they are impeded or obstructed by bodily thoughts (lines 10–12 and 15 ff.). This 'interference' which the intellect suffers from the body is a familiar theme in Descartes' work. Compare CB 1, where we are told how 'men of the senses' (*homines sensuales*) have only a confused grasp of the ideas present inside them from birth. At CB 9, a comparison is made with 'men who are half asleep' (*homines semisomnolenti*, line 21); the mind is submerged or swamped inside the body (*immersa*, lines 11 and 22)—a metaphor which also occurs in the *Principles* (I, 47). And the same general idea is expressed at *Principles* I, 71: 'In early childhood our mind was so closely bound to the body that it was filled simply with the thoughts by means of which it felt what was happening to the body, and had no time for any others.'

The fact that the *Principles* (1644) takes essentially the same line as that presented to Burman suggests that the 'present but submerged' solution represented Descartes' official position; while the 'dispositional' account offered to

Regius was more of an aberration.[1] This is strongly confirmed by the letter to 'Hyperaspistes' written in 1641, which uses language strikingly similar to that of the *Conversation*. The relevant passage (AT iii. 424) is worth quoting at length:

We know by experience that our minds are so closely joined to our bodies as to be almost always acted upon by them; and though in an adult and healthy body the mind enjoys some liberty to think of other things than those presented by the senses, we know there is not the same liberty in those who are sick or asleep or very young; and the younger they are the less liberty they have. So if one may conjecture on such an unexplored topic, it seems most reasonable to think that a mind newly united to an infant's body is wholly occupied in perceiving or feeling the ideas of pain, pleasure, heat, cold and other similar ideas which arise from its union and intermingling with the body. Nonetheless, it has in itself the ideas of God, itself, and all such truths as are called self-evident, in the same way as adult humans have when they are not attending to them; it does not acquire these ideas later on, as it grows older. I have no doubt that if it were taken out of the prison of the body it would find them within itself. (trans. follows Kenny: K 111)

There seems no doubt that this picture, drawn in such meticulous detail, and corresponding so closely to that presented in the *Principles* and the *Conversation*, represents the substance of Descartes' theory of innate ideas and their place in human development. Interestingly enough, the picture is almost exactly the opposite of that drawn in Wordsworth's famous ode. It is in infancy, when the demands of the body are most pressing, that the shades of the prison house are most tightly closed around us. As we grow up, and the signals from the body become less peremptory and obstructive, the ideas we are born with are allowed freer scope to make themselves felt.

---

[1] This is not the only place in the *Notes* where the line taken by Descartes appears to be inconsistent with his normal position. In another passage (referred to by Burman at CB 49) Descartes observes that 'in no case are ideas of things provided by the senses in the form in which we fashion them in our thought' (AT viiib. 358). Burman interprets Descartes as meaning to assert here that all ideas are innate, which would contradict the famous division of ideas into innate and adventitious in the Third Meditation. But Descartes makes it clear in his reply to Burman (lines 6–8, qq.v.) that he still holds to a genuine class of adventitious ideas. (For a different interpretation see KENNY (1), p. 105.)

A further development

The problem of infant knowledge is returned to at CB 49, where Burman asks whether the idea of the Trinity is innate. The example is well taken. *God* is one of the concepts listed by Descartes as innate along with mind, body, and a triangle (AT iii. 303, *et passim*). Now it may (perhaps) be plausible to suppose that the idea of a triangle is in some sense 'inside' a child; but it seems to stretch things a little too far to suppose that there is also inside him, waiting to emerge, the highly sophisticated concept of the Three-in-One and One-in-Three. In his reply to Burman, Descartes seems at first to be retreating into the old escape route of potentiality: 'even though the idea . . . is not innate in us to the extent of giving us an express representation of the Trinity, none the less the elements and rudiments of the idea are innate in us' (etiam si illa idea tam expresse, ut nobis Trinitatem repraesentet, innata non sit, ejus t[ame]n elementa et rudimenta nobis innata sunt) (CB 49, lines 9–12). Descartes does not, however, mean by this that the idea of the Trinity is present in rudimentary form—as a potentiality. Closer examination reveals that he is in effect making a distinction between simple and complex ideas. The idea of the Trinity is a complex idea, built up amongst other things of the idea of God and the idea of the number three. It is these latter, more simple ideas which are innate, and are the elements out of which the complex idea of the Trinity is built up, at a later date (ibid., lines 13–16).

The theological character of the example should not blind us to an important insight here which helps the innatist to escape from the dilemma we started with. The dilemma was between, on the one hand, attributing to a child ready-made explicit knowledge of, for example, Euclid's forty-third theorem, which risks making the theory just plain false; and, on the other hand, talking of 'potential knowledge of' or 'a disposition to acquire' the theorem, which risks making the theory vague and ultimately trivial. The new suggestion is that we should regard only certain basic 'rudimentary' or 'elemental' ideas as innate (in this case, perhaps, the basic concepts presupposed by Euclidean geometry). These are the logical building blocks out of which the more advanced truths, like the forty-third theorem, are later constructed, no doubt with the aid of sensory stimuli. The suggestion of course falls very far short of solving all the problems of innatism; nor is it without problems of its own: it is not going to be at all easy, for example, to specify exactly *which* are the elemental concepts and truths we are born with. But none the less an important step has been taken towards making the theory both more precise and less obviously implausible. Finally, the new development enlarges the scope of innatism in an important way: the phenomenon of *learning*, the fact that the growing child gradually acquires and builds up *new* concepts, now stands a chance of being accommodated within the theory instead of being politely ignored.

(iv) *Freedom and the will*

The existence of human freedom was axiomatic for Descartes. 'La liberté de notre volonté se connait sans preuve', he asserts in the *Principles* (I, 39). That our will is free is 'one of the first and most common notions which are innate in us' (ibid.). In the *Conversation*, Descartes supports his position by an appeal to inner experience. We have to go down deep into ourselves, Descartes tells Burman, and we will just see that our will is as perfect as it can be (CB 31, line 27); we can imagine beings cleverer than us, but not having a more perfect will. We have inner awareness of our freedom (intime conscii sumus nostrae libertatis) (CB 32, line 11).

But all this leaves unclear the precise nature and scope of the freedom Descartes believes in. At CB 32, Burman refers to the will as 'autonomous and indifferent' (*sui juris . . . & indifferens*). The term 'freedom of indifference' was traditionally used in the Schools to connote a completely independent or contra-causal power of the will ('which means a negation of causes', as Hume put it: *Treatise*, Bk. II, Part 3, ii). This view of our freedom is implied in the *Principles*, where Descartes speaks of our being conscious of the 'freedom and indifference which is inside us' (I, 41); in the same passage he says that the power of God has left the actions of men 'entirely free and undetermined' (entièrement libres et indéterminées).

A snag with this interpretation is that in the Fourth Meditation Descartes describes indifference as the 'lowest grade of liberty': 'the indifference that I am aware of when there is no reason that urges me one way rather than the other is the lowest grade of liberty: it is not evidence of any perfection in the will . . .' (AT vii. 58; HR i. 175). And later on there is the suggestion that the degree of true freedom is in inverse proportion to the degree of indifference (tanto magis sponte et libere illud credidi quanto minus fui ad istud ipsum indifferens) (AT vii. 59). However, the difficulty here is only apparent. For, as Descartes himself was later explicitly to admit, the sense in which he uses the term 'indifference' in the passages just quoted is a special one: the word is used to refer to the situation where one has no particular reason for taking either of two alternative courses of action; or where, in Descartes' own words, 'the will is not impelled one way rather than another by any perception of truth or goodness'.[1] This is like the situation of Buridan's ass, equidistant from two equally lush meadows (cf. Leibniz, *Theodicy*, Bk. I, § 49). The use of the term 'indifference' to characterize such a choice-situation corresponds to the modern English idiom: one might say, 'I am entirely indifferent as to which alternative to select—it makes no difference, as far as I can see.' This sense occurs at one point in the *Conversation*: in the pursuit of good and evil, says Descartes, indifference is a *fault*, since 'the will . . . ought to seek after the good without any indifference' (CB 32, lines 13–16). The 'fault' here must be not the autonomous power of the will, but a state of neutrality, of 'not caring either way'. So, the fact that Descartes refers slightingly to 'indifference' in the modern ('Buridan's ass') sense does not necessarily prevent us from taking him to be committed to freedom of indifference in the traditional (contra-causal) sense, and to be affirming such a commitment in the passage already quoted from the *Principles*.

However, a further problem arises in a remarkable passage in the *Conversation*. At CB 50, where the vexed issues of predestination, divine immutability, and grace are raised,

---

[1] 'Statum illum in quo est voluntas cum a nulla veri vel boni perceptione in unam magis quam in alteram partem impellitur.' Descartes adds: 'sed fortasse ab aliis per indifferentiam intellegitur positiva facultas se determinandi ad utrumlibet e duobus contrariis . . . quam positiam facultatem non negavi esse in voluntate'. (AT iv. 173; K 159. The date and recipient of this letter are in doubt.)

Descartes says that 'after weighing the truth of the matter, [he] finds himself in agreement with the Gomarists, rather than the Arminians or even, amongst his brethren, the Jesuits' (lines 36–9). In the fierce controversy following the death of Calvin, which is referred to here, Francis Gomar (1563–1641) had represented rigid adherence to strict predestinarianism, while Jacobus Arminius (1560–1609) took a more moderate position, holding that the sovereignty of God was compatible with a measure of human freedom. In affirming his preference for Gomarism, Descartes is, as he himself notes, putting himself at odds with some of his own Catholic brethren, notably the Jesuits. On the issues of predestination, the Jesuits had favoured the position of Luis de Molina (1535–1600), who had stressed the role played in salvation by free and independent (though divinely foreseen) co-operation with the grace of God; this was in contrast to the Jansenist doctrine of the irresistibility of divine grace.

The upshot of this is that Descartes' view, as stated in the *Conversation*, seems to involve an outright rejection of Molinism, and a denial of full-blooded human autonomy, or freedom of indifference. Indeed, if strict predestination is true, and divine grace completely irresistible, then it would seem that human freedom must reduce, at best, to mere spontaneity.

Despite this, there is an earlier text where Descartes' position seems much closer to that of Molina and the Jesuits. This is the famous analogy of the king and the duellists: a king orders two subjects who hate each other to be at a certain place at a certain time, knowing that nothing will stop them fighting; but 'for all that, he does not compel them, and his knowledge and even his will to make them act in this way (*les y déterminer*) does not prevent their fighting, when they meet, as freely and voluntarily as if they had met on another occasion without his knowledge . . . (AT iv. 353; K 189; letter to Elizabeth of January 1646). As Étienne Gilson has shown, Descartes' stressing of the real independence of the duellists does seem to favour a position more compatible with the Molinists', as against the stricter 'irresistibility' doctrine of the Jansenists. Faced with this apparently flat contradiction between the remarks in the *Conversation* and the letter to Elizabeth, Gilson concluded that Descartes took no fixed stand on the problem of human freedom, and was apt to speak at random when pressed on the subject.[1]

It seems to me, however, that this fails to take account of the special context of the passage in the *Conversation*. What is essentially at issue at CB 50 is not the freedom of men but the nature of God: in particular, God's indivisibility (his decrees are inseparable from himself: line 16) and his 'immutability' (he can undergo no change or alteration: line 42). Now it is well known that the omnipotence of God, in the Cartesian system, is quite absolute and unqualified (compare the divine control over even the eternal verities: CB 33). So we might well expect Descartes to argue that nothing can be allowed to detract from the supremely perfect and immutable divine nature. And this is just what happens at CB 50. We cannot, insists Descartes, think of God as changing his decrees in response to the prayers of men. Instead, we must think of him as having decreed from eternity to grant a given request, on condition that the petitioner is living a worthy life at the time (lines 28 ff.). It is in this respect and this respect only, then, that Descartes sides with the Gomarists as against the Arminians and Jesuits, viz. that the Gomarists have the most absolute and exalted view of the eternal sovereignty and immutability of God. Descartes never says, it should be noted, that this affects his conception of human freedom; indeed, human freedom is never mentioned at all at CB 50. And Descartes' constant refusal to compromise his philosophy by a rigid adherence to any one theological sect should make us wary of foisting on him acceptance of all the tenets of the Gomarists, just because of his agreement with them on a single point.

But surely, it will be objected, in siding with the Gomarists and acknowledging the complete sovereignty and immutability of the divine will, Descartes must, as a corollary of this, accept a downgrading of his conception of human freedom. But this line of reasoning (obviously implicit in Gilson's argument) is mistaken. The logical tension between

---

[1] 'Il [Descartes] défend selon les circonstances n'importe quelle solution, et encore ne se résigne-t-il à en défendre une que contraint et forcé par l'insistance de ses interlocuteurs' (GILSON (3), p. 394; cf. GIBSON, p. 339).

complete divine pre-ordination and genuine human freedom, acute though it is, is something Descartes consistently refused to be bothered by. He simply regarded the resolution of the problem as a *magnum mysterium*—something which, like the Incarnation, we have to accept on faith.[1] This comes out explicitly in the *Principles* (I, 40): 'Our knowledge of God leads us to perceive so immense a power in him that we think it impious to suppose anything could be done by us which has not been already pre-ordained by him. Now it is easy to get ourselves into great difficulty if we try to reconcile this divine pre-ordination with our freedom of the will, or grasp both at once' (AT viii. 20). A similar mystery surrounds the acts of God himself, as is made clear later on in CB 50. For although the acts of God are completely necessary (since he necessarily wills what is best), they are still completely free and 'indifferent': 'non deberet hic sejungi necessitas & indifferentia in Dei decretis, et quamvis maxime indifferenter egerit, simul tamen maxime necessario egit' (lines 48 ff.). Descartes concludes, as well he might, with a warning against trying to unravel this logical tangle: we must never allow ourselves the indulgence of trying to subject the nature and workings of God to our own reasoning (lines 59 ff.).

This description of God as 'acting with maximum indifference' is important in view of Descartes' frequent comparison between human and divine will. In the Fourth Meditation he makes the claim that our will, considered formally and precisely in itself, is as great as that of God (AT vii. 57). This claim is elaborated in the *Conversation*: any apparent imperfection in the will arises from errors in our understanding (which, of course, is far inferior to God's); the will itself is perfect (CB 31). Though Descartes' position on the nature of our freedom perhaps cannot be made fully consistent, these passages strongly suggest that he belongs with the partisans of full-blooded libertarian free will, or 'freedom of indifference'. However much of a mystery it may be, our actions are, for Descartes, 'entirely free and undetermined'.

---

[1] Compare a remark in *Cogitationes Privatae*, written as early as 1619: 'tria mirabilia fecit Dominus: res ex nihilo, liberum arbitrium, et Hominem Deum' (AT x. 218).

DESCARTES'
CONVERSATION
WITH
BURMAN

The replies of René Descartes to certain difficulties arising out of his *Meditations*, etc. Obtained directly from the author.

Egmond, 16 April 1648

[Meditations and Replies to Objections]

MEDIT. I

[1]   p. 8: Whatever I have so far accepted as most true I have acquired *either from the senses or through the senses.*

[AT vii. 18; HR i. 145]

From the senses: i.e. from sight, by which I have perceived colours, shapes, and such like. Leaving aside sight, however, I have acquired everything else *through the senses,* i.e. through hearing; for this is how I acquired and gleaned what I know, from my parents, teachers, and others.   5

The objection cannot be made here that this leaves out the common principles and ideas of God and of ourselves, which were never in the senses (*Med.*, p. 34). For, firstly, I acquired these in the same way, *through the senses,* that is to say, through hearing. Secondly, the author is considering at this   10
point the man who is only just beginning to philosophize, and who is paying attention only to what he knows he is aware of. As regards the common principles and axioms, for example 'it is impossible that one and the same thing should both be and not be', men who are creatures of the senses, as   15
we all are at a pre-philosophical level, do not think about these or pay attention to them. On the contrary, since they are present in us from birth with such clarity, and since we experience them inside ourselves, we neglect them and think about them only in a confused manner, but never in the   20
abstract, or apart from material things and particular instances. Indeed, if people were to think about these principles in the abstract, no one would have any doubt about them; and if the Sceptics had done this, no one would ever have been a Sceptic; for they cannot be denied by any-   25
one who carefully focuses his attention on them. Thirdly, here we are dealing primarily with the question of whether anything has real existence.

3

[2]   p. 13: *I will suppose therefore* that not God (who is supremely
       good and the source of truth) but rather some malignant
       demon of the utmost power and cunning has employed all his
       energies in order to deceive me.
                                              [AT vii. 22; HR i. 148]

The author is here making us as doubtful as he can and cast-
ing us into as many doubts as possible. This is why he raises
not only the customary difficulties of the Sceptics but every
difficulty that can possibly be raised; the aim is in this way to
demolish completely every single doubt. And this is the   5
purpose behind the introduction at this point of the demon,
which some might criticize as a superfluous addition.

[3]   *of the utmost power*
                                                          [ibid.]

What the author here says is contradictory, since malice is
incompatible with supreme power.

[4]   p. 155: But when we take note of the fact that we are thinking
       beings, this is a primary notion, which is not derived *from any
       syllogism*.
                               [Second Replies: AT vii. 140; HR ii. 38]

   [O.] But is not the opposite asserted at *Principles* I, 10?
   R. Before this inference, 'I think therefore I am', the major
'whatever thinks is' can be known; for it is in reality prior
to my inference, and my inference depends on it. This is why
the author says in the *Principles* that the major premiss comes   5
first, namely because implicitly it is always presupposed and
prior. But it does not follow that I am always expressly and
explicitly aware of its priority, or that I know it before my
inference. This is because I am attending only to what I
experience inside myself—for example, 'I think therefore   10
I am': I do not pay attention in the same way to the general
notion 'whatever thinks is'. As I have explained before, we
do not separate out these general propositions from the
particular instances; rather, it is *in* the particular instances
that we think of them. This then is the sense in which the   15
words from page 155 cited here should be taken.

[5]   p. 474: As for the assertion that it is self-contradictory that men
should be deceived by God, this is clearly demonstrated from
the fact that the form of deception is non-being, *towards which
supreme being cannot incline.*

[Sixth Replies: AT vii. 428; HR ii. 245]

As far as we are concerned, since we are composed partly of
nothingness and partly of being, we incline partly towards
being and partly towards nothingness. As for God, on the
other hand, he cannot incline to nothingness, since he is
supreme and pure being. This consideration is a meta-   5
physical one and is perfectly clear to all those who give their
mind to it. Hence, inasmuch as I have my faculty of perception from God, and in so far as I use it correctly, by
assenting only to what I clearly perceive, I cannot be
deceived or tricked by it; if I were, God would have to   10
incline to nothingness. For this would be a case of God's
deceiving me and so tending to non-being.

[O.] Someone, however, may still raise the following
objection: after I have proved that God exists and is not a
deceiver, then I can say that my mind certainly does not   15
deceive me, since a reliable mind was God's gift to me;
but my memory may still deceive me since I may think I
remember something which I do not in fact remember.
This is because of the weakness of memory.

R. I have nothing to say on the subject of memory. Every-   20
one should test himself to see whether he is good at
remembering. If he has any doubts, then he should make use
of written notes and so forth to help him.

[6]   p. 283: *Lastly, as to the fact that* I was not guilty of *circularity* when
I said that the only reason we have for being sure that what we
clearly and distinctly perceive is true is the fact that God exists;
but that we are sure God exists only because we perceive this
clearly: I have already given an adequate explanation of this
point in the reply to the Second Objections, Nos. 3 and 4,
where I made a distinction between what we in fact perceive
clearly and what we remember having perceived clearly.

[Fourth Replies: AT vii. 245; HR ii. 114]

[O.] It seems there is a circle. For in the Third Meditation
the author uses axioms to prove the existence of God, even

though he is not yet certain of not being deceived about these.

R. He does use such axioms in the proof, but he knows 5 that he is not deceived with regard to them, since he is actually paying attention to them. And for as long as he does pay attention to them, he is certain that he is not being deceived, and he is compelled to give his assent to them.

[O.] But our mind can think of only one thing at a time, 10 whereas the proof in question is a fairly long one involving several axioms. Then again, every thought occurs instantaneously, and there are many thoughts which come to mind in the proof. So one will not be able to keep the attention on all the axioms, since any one thought will get in the way of 15 another.

R. Firstly, it is just not true that the mind can think of only one thing at a time. It is true that it cannot think of a large number of things at the same time, but it can still think of more than one thing. For example, I am now aware 20 and have the thought that I am talking and that I am eating; and both these thoughts occur at the same time. Then, secondly, it is false that thought occurs instantaneously; for all my acts take up time, and I can be said to be continuing and carrying on with the same thought during a period of 25 time.

[O.] But on that showing, our thought will be extended and divisible.

R. Not at all. Thought will indeed be extended and divisible with respect to its duration, since its duration can 30 be divided into parts. But it is not extended and divisible with respect to its nature, since its nature remains unextended. It is just the same with God: we can divide his duration into an infinite number of parts, even though God himself is not therefore divisible. 35

[O.] But eternity is all at once and once for all (*simul et semel*).

R. That is impossible to conceive of. It is all at once and once for all, in so far as nothing is ever added to or taken away from the nature of God. But it is not all at once and 40 once for all in the sense that it exists all at once (*simul*). For since we can divide it up now, after the creation of the world, why should it not have been possible to do the same

before creation, since duration remains constant? Thus,
eternity has now coexisted with created things for, say,   45
five thousand years, and has occupied time along with them:
so it could have done just the same before creation, if we
had had some standard to measure it by.

Accordingly, since our thought is able to grasp more than
one item in this way, and since it does not occur instan-   50
taneously, it is clear that we are able to grasp the proof of
God's existence in its entirety. As long as we are engaged in
this process, we are certain that we are not being deceived,
and every difficulty is thus removed.

[7]   *The fact that there can be nothing in the mind,* in so far as it is a
      thinking thing, of which it is not aware, seems to me self-
      evident.
                              [ibid.: AT vii. 246; HR ii. 115]

[O.] But how can it be aware, since to be aware is itself a
thought? In order to have the thought that you are aware,
you must move on to another thought; if you do this, you
can no longer be thinking of the thing you were thinking
of a moment ago. It follows that you cannot be aware that   5
you *are* thinking, but only that you *were* thinking.

R. It is correct that to be aware is both to think and to
reflect on one's thought. But it is false that this reflection
cannot occur while the previous thought is still there. This is
because, as we have already seen, the soul is capable of   10
thinking of more than one thing at the same time, and of
continuing with a particular thought which it has. It has
the power to reflect on its thoughts as often as it likes, and
to be aware of its thought in this way.

[8]   For we can conceive of nothing in the mind, regarded in this
      way, that is not a thought or *dependent on a thought.*
                                                      [ibid.]

For example, the movement of the arm.

In view of this I do not doubt that the mind begins to think as soon
as it is implanted in the body of an infant.

[ibid.]

[O.] The author of these objections conjectured that it
would follow from this that the mind must always be
thinking, even in the case of infants.

R. The author agreed.

[O.] But since we have an innate idea of God and of our- 5
selves, would not the mind of an infant therefore have an
actual idea of God?

R. It would be rash to maintain that, since we have no
evidence relevant to the point. It does not, however, seem
probable that this is so. For in infancy the mind is so 10
swamped inside the body that the only thoughts it has are
those which result from the way the body is affected.

[O.] But the mind can think of more than one thing at
once.

R. It can, provided that one thought does not obstruct 15
another, which is what happens in this case. The body has
an obstructive effect on the soul. We are aware of this
phenomenon in ourselves, when we prick ourselves with a
needle or some sharp instrument: the effect is such that we
cannot think of anything else. It is the same with men who 20
are half asleep: they can scarcely think of more than one
thing. In infancy, therefore, the mind was so swamped inside
the body that it could think only of bodily matters. The
body is always a hindrance to the mind in its thinking, and
this was especially true in youth. 25

As to the fact that we have no memory of the thoughts we
had in infancy, this is because no traces of these thoughts
have been imprinted on the brain, like this. . . . By the same
token, there are many thoughts we had yesterday, etc.,
which we cannot now remember. But the mind cannot ever 30
be without thought; it can of course be without this or that
thought, but it cannot be without *some* thought. In the same
way, the body cannot, even for a moment, be without
extension.

[O.] But even if traces are not imprinted on the brain, so 35
that there is no bodily memory, there still exists an intellectual memory, as undoubtedly is the case with angels or

disembodied souls, for example. And this intellectual
memory ought to enable the mind to remember its thoughts.

R. I do not refuse to admit intellectual memory: it does 40
exist. When, for example, on hearing that the word
'K-I-N-G' signifies supreme power, I commit this to my
memory and then subsequently recall the meaning by means
of my memory, it must be the intellectual memory that makes
this possible. For there is certainly no relationship between 45
the four letters (K-I-N-G) and their meaning, which would
enable me to derive the meaning from the letters. It is the
intellectual memory that enables me to recall what the
letters stand for. However, this intellectual memory has
universals rather than particulars as its objects, and so it 50
cannot enable us to recall every single thing we have done.

MEDIT. II

[10]   p. 18: But what am I to say now, when I am supposing that
           there is some deceiver who is supremely powerful *and, if it is*
           permissible to say so, malicious?
                                        [AT vii. 26; HR i. 151]

The restriction is added here because the author is saying
something contradictory in using the phrase 'supremely
powerful and malicious', since supreme power cannot co-
exist with malice. This is why he says 'if it is permissible to
say so'.   5

[11]   p. 21: Now in all this, even though I may be permanently
           asleep, and even though *he who created me* deceives me as much
           as he can, is there anything which is not just as true as the fact
           of my existence?
                                        [AT vii. 29; HR i. 153]

But is it God who created me? For all I know, may not that
demon who tricked me be the one who created me? At this
point, however, I have not yet attained any knowledge
about these matters, and I am speaking of them only in a
confused manner.   5

[12] p. 25: Or do I not rather perceive the nature of the wax better now, after a more careful investigation *both of what it is* and of the way in which it is known.

[AT vii. 32; HR i. 156]

The author made this investigation in the preceding section, where he examined all the attributes and accidents of the wax. He gradually saw all these attributes leave the wax, and others take their places.

[13] p. 421: Here, as frequently elsewhere, you merely show that you do not sufficiently understand what you attempt to criticize. *For I did not abstract* the concept of the wax from that of its accidents.

[Fifth Replies: AT vii. 359; HR ii. 212]

[O.] But the author seems to have done just that in this very Meditation, when he showed that the accidents leave the wax, which amounts to showing that the actual body or substance of the wax remains.

R. None the less the author did not make the abstraction. For although he conceded and stated that these accidents, such as hardness, cold, and so on, leave the wax, he also stated and expressly remarked that others always replace them, so that the wax is never without accidents. So at no point did the author abstract the wax from its accidents. 10

[14] p. 254: But a created mind, even though it may perhaps really possess adequate knowledge of many things, can never know that it does so. . . . For in order to know it possessed this knowledge . . . it would have to *equal the infinite capacity of God* in its power of knowing: and this is quite impossible.

[Fourth Replies: AT vii. 220; HR ii. 97]

[O.] Why should this be necessary, since God has of his own accord limited this power in his creatures, so that we should have no need to equal his infinite power?

R. We do not know this. For example, let us take a triangle. This appears to be something extremely simple, which it seems we should very easily be able to achieve adequate knowledge of. Yet, none the less, we cannot do so. Even if we prove that it possesses all the attributes we can

conceive of, none the less after, say, a thousand years
another mathematician may detect further properties in it. 10
It follows that we will never be certain that we have
grasped everything that could have been grasped about it.
The same can be said with regard to the body, and its
extension, and everything else. As for the author, he has
never attributed to himself adequate knowledge of any 15
thing whatsoever; but none the less he is certain that in many,
if not all, cases, he has the sort of knowledge and the sort of
foundations from which adequate knowledge could be—and
perhaps already has been—deduced. But who can say?

MEDIT. III

[15]   p. 31: For certainly if I considered the ideas merely as certain
         modes of my thought, without referring them to anything
         else, they could *scarcely* give *me any* subject-matter for error.
                                          [AT vii. 37; HR i. 160]

[O.] But since all error concerning ideas comes from their
relation and application to external things, there seems to be
no subject-matter for error whatsoever if they are not
referred to externals.
   R. Even if I do not refer my ideas to anything outside 5
myself, there is still subject-matter for error, since I can
make a mistake with regard to the actual nature of the ideas.
For example, I may consider the idea of colour, and say that
it is a thing or a quality; or I may say that the colour itself,
which is represented by this idea, is something of the kind. 10
For example, I may say whiteness is a colour; and even if I
do not refer this idea to anything outside myself—even if
I do not say or suppose that there is any white thing—I may
still make a mistake in the abstract, with regard to whiteness
itself and its nature or the idea I have of it.   15

[16]   p. 33: *So perhaps* there is in me some other faculty, not yet fully
         known to me, which produces these ideas [of external things].
                                          [AT vii. 39; HR i. 161]

[O.] But I have already come to know that I am a thinking
thing; and I know that these ideas cannot come from a
thinking thing.

11

[R] But, firstly, this is only an objection and a doubt that could be raised. Secondly, I am not at this point con- 5 centrating on my nature to the extent to which I do subsequently when I reflect on it. Indeed, neither in the First Meditation nor anywhere in the Second did I do this. But subsequently, a little later on in this Third Meditation when I reflect a little more carefully about myself, I solve 10 this problem.

[17]   p. 37: If, on the other hand, no such idea can be found in me, *I shall simply have no* argument to convince me of the existence of a being apart from myself.

                                   [AT vii. 42; HR i. 163]

[O.] But is there not another argument later on in the Fifth Meditation?

R. At this point the author is speaking of the sort of argument that can take some effect of God as a premiss from which the existence of a supreme cause, namely God, can 5 subsequently be inferred. In fact, however, he discovered no such effect: after a most careful survey of all the effects, he found none which would serve to prove God's existence except for the idea of God. By contrast, the other argument in the Fifth Meditation proceeds *a priori* and does not start 10 from some effect. In the *Meditations* that argument comes later than the one here; the fact that it comes later, while the proof in this Meditation comes first, is the result of the order in which the author discovered the two proofs. In the *Principles*, however, he reverses the order; for the method 15 and order of discovery is one thing, and that of exposition another. In the *Principles* his purpose is exposition, and his procedure is synthetic.

[18]   p. 39: *And since there can be no ideas which are not as it were of things* . . .

                                   [AT vii. 44; HR i. 164]

[O.] But we have an idea of nothing, and this is not an idea of a thing.

R. That idea is purely negative, and can hardly be called

an idea. In this passage the author is taking the word 'idea'
in its strict and narrow sense. We do also have ideas of   5
common notions, which are not, strictly speaking, ideas of
things. But this is a rather extended use of the word 'idea'.

[19]   p. 41: I clearly understand . . . that my conception of the
        infinite, that is, God, is prior to my conception of the finite,
        that is, myself. *For how could I understand that I doubted* and
        desired—that is, lacked something—or that I was not com-
        pletely perfect, unless there were in me some idea of a more
        perfect being, which enabled me to recognize my own defects
        by comparison?
                                              [AT vii. 45; HR i. 166]

[O.] But in the *Discourse*, p. 31, the author says he has seen
most clearly that knowledge was a greater sign of perfection
than doubt. He must, then, have known this without
reference to the perfect being; and so it is not the case that
his knowledge of God was prior to the knowledge of   5
himself.

R. In that part of the *Discourse* you have a summary of
these *Meditations*, and its meaning must be explicated by
reference to the *Meditations* themselves. In that part of the
Discourse, then, the author recognized his own imperfection   10
by recognizing the perfection of God. He did this implicitly if not explicitly. Explicitly, we are able to recognize
our own imperfection before we recognize the perfection of
God. This is because we are able to direct our attention to
ourselves before we direct our attention to God. Thus we   15
can infer our own finiteness before we arrive at his infinite-
ness. Despite this, however, the knowledge of God and his
perfection must *implicitly* always come before the knowledge
of ourselves and our imperfections. For in reality the
infinite perfection of God is prior to our imperfections,   20
since our imperfection is a defect and negation of the
perfection of God. And every defect and negation presupposes that which it falls short and negates.

[O.] But in that case nothingness would have to presuppose being, would it not?   25

R. In Metaphysics our understanding of nothingness
derives from that of being.

[20] p. 42: For I experience already a gradual increase in knowledge; and I see no reason why . . . *through its help I should not be able* to acquire all the other perfections of God.

[AT vii. 47; HR i. 167]

[*O*.] But how can knowledge contribute to the acquisition of all the other perfections of God?

R. It can do so to a very great extent. It is by knowledge that we become wiser and more prudent and know the other perfections more clearly. Once we know them clearly, we 5 will acquire them all the more easily, since wisdom and prudence will be able to provide us with the means for their acquisition.

[21] p. 44: Had I been the author of my own existence . . . I should certainly not have denied myself any of the things which are rather easy to acquire (i.e. many forms of knowledge which I lack); nor indeed should I have denied myself any of the other things which I see are contained in the idea of God, since *none of them seem to me to be any more difficult* to acquire.

[AT vii. 48; HR i. 168]

Now here one must carefully distinguish between *understanding, conception,* and *imagination*—a distinction of great value. Take for example the perfections of God. We do not *imagine* these, or *conceive* of them, but we *understand* them: the way in which God understands all things in a single mental 5 act, or the way in which his decrees are identical with himself, are things which we *understand*, but we do not *conceive of*, since we cannot, so to speak, represent them to ourselves. Thus, we *understand* the perfections and attributes of God, but we do not *conceive of* them—or, rather, in order to con- 1c ceive of them, we conceive of them as indefinite. Now, if it were I who had given myself my nature and make-up, I would have given myself all the perfections of God. And I think I would have given myself these perfections in accordance with my indefinite conception of them. For example, I 1: would have given myself greater knowledge than I now possess; and when I had that greater knowledge, I would then have given myself greater knowledge still, and so on. Now when indefinites are multiplied in this way they become infinite: or rather they become *the* infinite, since the 2c

infinite is the same as the indefinite multiplied in this way.
As I increased my knowledge more and more in this way,
I would by the same token have increased my other attributes
(I do not think these would prove any harder than knowledge, since it is by means of knowledge that they are to be   25
attained), and I would end up as God. As it is, however, I
know by experience that I cannot do this and am unable to
increase my knowledge as I should like to. It follows that
I do not derive my existence from myself, etc.

[22]   p. 186: *It is a greater thing to create or conserve a substance than* to
           create or conserve *the attributes* or properties of a substance.
                                       [Second Replies: AT vii. 166; HR ii. 57]

That is, 'than to create or conserve the attributes of *that same*
substance'. One must not here start comparing one substance with the attributes of another.
   [O.] But surely the attributes are the same as the substance.
So it cannot be 'a greater thing' to create the substance, etc.   5
   R. It is true that the attributes are the same as the substance, but this is when they are all taken together, not when
they are taken individually, one by one. So it is a greater
thing to produce a substance than its attributes, if by producing all the attributes you mean producing each one   10
individually, one after the other.

[23]   p. 45 : Nor can I escape the force of these arguments if I suppose
           that I have always existed as I now do, *as though it followed from
           this supposition* that there was no need to look for any author
           of my existence.
                                       [AT vii. 48; HR i. 168]

   [O.] But surely it *does* follow, in the view of those who say
that there can be nothing created from all eternity, citing as
proof the fact that it would then be independent, like God
himself.
   R. Well, that is their view. As far as I am concerned, I do   5
not see why God should not have been able to create something from eternity. Since God possessed his power from all
eternity, I do not see any reason why he should not have
been able to exercise it from all eternity.

[O.] But a free cause is conceived of as prior to its effects 10
and its purposes.

R. But then it would have to follow that the decrees of
God did not exist from eternity, especially since power and
creation do not presuppose a greater action in God than
his decrees. What is more, decrees are acts of will, and so 15
must the creation be, since it is merely the will of God. If it
were anything else, the creation would involve something
new happening to God.

[O.] But then we would have an infinite number.

R. What is absurd about that? Do we not get the same 20
when we divide a quantity? People try to make a distinction
here, but it is vacuous. And if you can have an infinite
number in future eternity, which is what we believe as an
article of faith, then why should not the same be true of past
eternity? 25

[O.] But in the case of past eternity, the divisions are actual
and all at once. But in future eternity, they are only in
potentiality, and are never all at once and in actuality.

R. The divisions in past eternity are not actualized all at
once, for there is only one division for which this is so, 30
namely the present. With respect to all the other divisions, it
is the same as it is with future eternity. If, then, the one sort
of eternity can exist, so can the other. Accordingly, if I
existed from eternity, the parts into which my duration is
divided would be separated, and they would none the less 35
depend on God. The argument thus retains its force. However, the author took express care to keep questions of this
sort out of his *Meditations*, so far as he was able, in order
to avoid giving any offence to the Schoolmen, and so on.

[24] p. 48: But the mere fact that God created me *is a very strong basis
for believing* that I am somehow made in his image and likeness.
[AT vii. 51; HR i. 170]
Compare also p. 436: For although the three modes of action
are quite different in kind, there *is less of a gap* between natural
production and divine, than there is between artificial and
divine.
[Fifth Replies: AT vii. 373; HR ii. 222]

[O.] But why do you say that? Surely God could have
created you without creating you in his image?

R. No. It is a common axiom and a true one that *the effect is like the cause*. Now God is the cause of me, and I am an effect of him, so it follows that I am like him.   5

[O.] But a builder is the cause of a house, yet for all that the house is not like him.

R. He is not the cause of the house, in the sense in which we are taking the word here. He merely applies active forces to what is passive, and so there is no need for the   10
product to be like the man. In this passage, however, we are talking about the total cause, the cause of being itself. Anything produced by *this* cause must necessarily be like it. For since the cause is itself being and substance, and it brings something into being, i.e. out of nothing (a method of pro-   15
duction which is the prerogative of God), what is produced must at the very least be being and substance. To this extent at least, it will be like God and bear his image.

[O.] But in that case even stones and such like are going to be in God's image.   20

R. Even these things do have the image and likeness of God, but it is very remote, minute and indistinct. As for me, on the other hand, God's creation has endowed me with a greater number of attributes, and so his image is in me to a greater extent. I am not, however, taking 'image' here in   25
the ordinary sense of an effigy or picture of something, but in the broader sense of something having some resemblance with something else. The reason I used these particular words in the *Meditations* was that throughout the Scriptures we are said to be created in the image of God.   30

[25]   p. 179: Substance: this term applies to *every thing in which* whatever we perceive is immediately located, as in a subject; or every thing by means of which whatever we perceive exists. By 'whatever we perceive' is meant any property, quality, or attribute which we have a real idea of.
                   [Second Replies: AT vii. 161; HR ii. 53]

In addition to the attribute which specifies the substance, one must think of the substance itself which is the substrate of that attribute. For example, since the mind is a thinking thing, there is in addition to the thinking a substance which does the thinking, and so on.   5

[26] p. 153: As for those who deny that they have the idea of God
but instead of it form *some idol* etc., while they refuse the name,
they concede the fact.

[Second Replies: AT vii. 139; HR ii. 37]

'Idol' is in fact their equivalent of our 'idea'. But in so far
as they form a real idea when they are forming the idol, the
idea they form is materially false.

[27] The conclusion is . . . that *I have the power* of conceiving that a
number is thinkable that is greater than any number that can
ever be thought of by me, and that I have received this power
not from myself but from some other entity more perfect than I.

[ibid.]

This argument could not have any force for an atheist, who
would not allow himself to be convinced by it. Indeed, it is
not suitable for this purpose, and the author does not wish it
to be understood in this way. It must rather be conjoined
with other arguments concerning God, since it pre- 5
supposes such arguments, and takes God's existence as
already proved by them. Thus, the author had already
proved the existence of God from the idea of God in this
part of the *Replies*, so the sense of this passage should
accordingly be as follows: 'I know God exists and have 10
proved it. At the same time, I notice that when I count I
can never reach a highest number, but there is always a
number that can be thought of, which is greater than any
number that I can think of. It follows that the power of conceiving of this is something I do not derive from myself, but 15
must have received from some entity more perfect than
myself. And this entity is God, whose existence I have
proved by means of the arguments already adduced.'

[28] p. 153: With regard to your further point *concerning the idea of an
angel*, than which we are less perfect, I readily admit that there
is certainly no need for this idea to have been produced in us
by an angel.

[ibid.: AT vii. 138; HR ii. 37]

As far as the idea of an angel goes, it is certain that we form
it from the idea we have of our own mind: this is the sole

source of our knowledge of it. And this is so true that we can think of nothing in an angel *qua* angel that we cannot also notice in ourselves.   5

[O.] But on this view, an angel is going to be identical with our mind, since each is something that merely thinks.

R. It is true that both are thinking things. But this still does not prevent an angel from having many more per-fections than our mind, or having perfections of a   10 higher degree. Indeed, it is possible that they may even differ in kind. Thus St. Thomas wanted every angel to be of a different kind from every other, and he described each one in as much detail as if he had been right in their midst, which is how he got the honorific title of the 'Angelic Doctor'. Yet   15 although he spent more time on this question than on almost anything else, nowhere were his labours more point-less. For knowledge about angels is virtually out of our reach, when we do not derive such knowledge from our own minds, as I have said. We just do not know the answers   20 to all the standard questions concerning angels, for example whether they can be united with a body, or what the bodies were like which they frequently took in the Old Testament, and so on. It is best for us to follow Scripture and believe they were young men, or appeared as such, and so forth.   25

MEDIT. IV

[29]   p. 53: *And for this reason alone* I consider that the customary search for final causes is totally useless in physics.
                         [AT vii. 55; HR i. 173]
        Compare also p. 438: *And we cannot pretend* that certain of God's purposes are more out in the open than others: all are equally hidden in the inscrutable abyss of his wisdom.
                         [Fifth Replies: AT vii. 375; HR ii. 223]

This rule—that we must never argue from ends—should be carefully heeded. For, firstly, the knowledge of a thing's purpose never leads us to a knowledge of the thing itself; its nature remains just as obscure to us. Indeed, this constant practice of arguing from ends is Aristotle's greatest fault.   5 Secondly, all the purposes of God are hidden from us, and it is rash to want to plunge into them. I am not speaking here of purposes which are known through revelation; it is

purely as a philosopher that I am considering them. It is here
that we go completely astray. We think of God as a sort of   10
superman, who thinks up such and such a scheme, and tries
to realize it by such-and-such means. This is clearly quite
unworthy of God.

[30]   p. 55 : *And from the very fact that I can form an idea of it* [a faculty
         of infinite understanding], I perceive that it belongs to the
         nature of God.
                                              [AT vii. 57; HR i. 174]

Since I know from my idea of God that he is the most
perfect being and that all absolute perfections belong to him,
I must attribute to him only what I know is absolutely
perfect. Now take any attribute that I can form an idea of as
meeting this requirement—anything I can think of as an   5
absolutely perfect perfection: from the very fact that I can
form an idea of it, I know that it belongs to the nature of
God.

[31]   For although God's will is incomparably greater than mine,
         both by reason of the knowledge and power that accompany
         it . . . and by reason of its object—by ranging over a greater
         number of items—it does *not, however*, seem any greater than
         mine when considered *formally* and precisely *in itself*.
                                                          [ibid.]

[*O.*] But when considered in this abstract way, understanding is understanding, and so our understanding too is
not going to differ from that of God, even though God's
understanding ranges over a greater number of objects.

    R. But understanding depends on its object and cannot be   5
separated from it; so it is not the case that 'understanding is
understanding'. Moreover, it is not just that our understanding ranges over fewer objects than that of God: rather,
it is extremely imperfect in itself, being obscure, mingled
with ignorance, and so on.   10

    [*O.*] But in that case our will too is imperfect. We will
one moment, and not the next; one moment we have a
volition, the next—when our will is imperfect—a mere
velleity.

R. That simply shows that there is a lack of constancy in 15
our volition, not that there is any imperfection in our will.
Each occurrence of the will is as perfect as the next: the
fluctuation you speak of has its origin in judgement, and is
due to the fact that our judgement is faulty.

[O.] But judgement itself is an operation of the will. 20

R. It is indeed an operation of the will, and as such it is
perfect. Every imperfection under which the judgement
labours comes from intellectual ignorance. If this were
removed, the fluctuation would disappear too, and our
judgement would be stable and perfect. But there is no point 25
in arguing like this on these matters. Let everyone just go
down deep into himself and find out whether or not he has
a perfect and absolute will, and whether he can conceive of
anything which surpasses him in freedom of the will. I am
sure everyone will find that it is as I say. It is in this, then, 30
that the will is greater and more godlike than the intellect.

[32]   p. 61: Moreover, although I do not have the power to avoid
       error in the first way mentioned (i.e. by being endowed with
       manifest perception of everything I have to deliberate on), *I can*
       avoid error *in the second way*, which depends merely on re-
       membering to withhold judgement on any matter where the
       truth is not clear.

[AT vii. 61; HR i. 178]

[O.] But in that case why should I not also have this ability
with regard to the pursuit of good and evil, or again with
regard to supernatural matters, since these things too
depend on the will, and the will is always autonomous and
indifferent? 5

R. We must leave the latter point for the theologians to
explain. For the philosopher, it is enough to study man as he
is now in his natural condition. I have written my philosophy in such a way as to make it acceptable anywhere—
even among the Turks—and to avoid giving the slightest 10
offence to anyone. Now we have inner consciousness of our
freedom, and we know that we can withhold our assent
when we wish. In the pursuit of good and evil, however,
when the will is indifferent with respect to each of the two,
it is already at fault, since it ought to seek after the good 15

alone without any indifference, in contrast to the situation in theoretical subjects. With regard to supernatural matters, the theologians teach that this is an area where we are corrupted through original sin: we need grace to enable us to recognize and pursue the good in this sphere. Indeed, 20 almost all sins have their source in ignorance, since no one can pursue evil *qua* evil. So it is through his grace that God has promised us eternal life—something no one would have thought of or ever aspired to—in return for those good works of ours which in any case we were bound to perform. 25 But it can be said that our will is corrupted by the emotions.

[33]   p. 479: For we cannot conceive that anything *is thought of in the divine intellect* as good or true, or worthy of belief or action or omission, until the will of God has decided to make it so.
[Sixth Replies: AT vii, 432; HR ii. 248]

[O.] But what then of God's ideas of possible things? Surely these are prior to his will.

R. These too depend on God, like everything else. His will is the cause not only of what is actual and to come, but also of what is possible and of the simple natures. There is 5 nothing we can think of or ought to think of that should not be said to depend on God.

[O.] But does it follow from this that God could have commanded a creature to hate him, and thereby made this a good thing to do? 10

R. God could not now do this: but we simply do not know what he could have done. In any case, why should he not have been able to give this command to one of his creatures?

MEDIT. V

[34]   p. 64: When, for example, I imagine a triangle, even though
no such figure exists, or has ever existed, anywhere outside my
thought, it still has a determinate nature or essence or form
which is immutable and eternal and not fictitious or dependent
on my mind; *as is clear from the fact that* various properties can
be demonstrated of the triangle.

[AT vii. 64; HR i. 180]

[O.] But since I can demonstrate various properties of a
chimera, on your view not even a chimera is going to be a
fictitious entity.

R. Everything in a chimera that can be clearly and distinctly conceived is a true entity. It is not fictitious, since it   5
has a true and immutable essence, and this essence comes
from God just as much as the actual essence of other things.
An entity is said to be 'fictitious', on the other hand, when it
is merely our supposition that it exists. Thus, all the
demonstrations of mathematicians deal with true entities   10
and objects, and the complete and entire object of Mathematics and everything it deals with is a true and real entity.
This object has a true and real nature, just as much as the
object of Physics itself. The only difference is that Physics
considers its object not just as a true and real entity, but also   15
as something actually and specifically existing. Mathematics,
on the other hand, considers its object merely as possible,
i.e. as something which does not actually exist in space but
is capable of doing so. It must be stressed at this point that
we are talking of clear perception, not of imagination. Even   20
though we can with the utmost clarity imagine the head of a
lion joined to the body of a goat, or some such thing, it does
not therefore follow that they exist, since we do not clearly
perceive the link, so to speak, which joins the parts together. For example, I may clearly see Peter standing, but I   25
do not clearly see that standing is contained in and conjoined with Peter. Now if we are accustomed to clear perceptions we will never have a false conception. As to
whether our perceptions are clear or not, this is something
we know perfectly well from our own inner awareness.   30
This is the point of all the explanations which the author
went through in Book One of the *Principles*, and it is of very
great benefit to be acquainted with them.

[35]   p. 68: There are many ways in which I realize that [my idea of
        God] . . . is the image of a true and immutable nature. First,
        there is no other thing I can think of such that existence belongs
        to its essence; second . . ., *I cannot intelligibly think of two or more*
        Gods of this sort.

                                                    [AT vii. 68; HR i. 182]

[O.] But why not, since they will still be Gods?

R. They would certainly not be Gods, since 'God' means
something such that absolutely every perfection is included
in it.

[O.] But this is true of God taken as a kind of thing, so to   5
speak, not as an individual; so that one God would not rule
out another in this way, any more than if one mind has all
the perfections of a mind, this rules out another mind.

[R.] But that is not a parallel argument. 'Mind' does not
signify absolutely every perfection, as 'God' does. This is   10
why these perfections can only be in one being. If there were
several beings, they would not be supreme, and so they
would not be God on pain of contradiction. There is, however, no inconsistency in the fact that there are three
Persons, since there is an identical essence, and they are one 15
God.

[36]   p. 125: *For we are* so *used* to distinguishing essence from exist-
        ence in the case of all other things, that we forget how in the
        case of God existence belongs to essence to a greater degree
        than in the case of other things.

                                        [First Replies: AT vii. 116; HR ii. 19]

[O.] But are we right to make the distinction? Is essence
then prior to existence? And, in creating things did God
merely give them existence?

R. We are right to separate the two in our thought, for we
can conceive of essence without actual existence, as in the
case of a rose in winter. However, the two cannot be
separated in reality in accordance with the customary
distinction; for there was no essence prior to existence,
since existence is merely existing essence. So one is really not
prior to the other, nor are they separate or distinct.   1

[37]   p. 169: For all contradictoriness or impossibility resides simply
         in our thought, when we make the mistake of joining together
         mutually inconsistent ideas: it cannot occur *in anything* which
         is outside the mind.
                                  [Second Replies: AT vii. 152; HR ii. 46]

[O.] But our ideas depend on real things. So if there is a
contradiction in our ideas, there will also be one in the things
themselves.

R. Our ideas do depend on things, in so far as they represent them. But none the less, there is no contradiction in   5
things, but in our ideas alone. For it is ideas alone that we
join together in such a way that they are inconsistent one
with another. Things, by contrast, are not inconsistent with
each other, since all of them can exist: so no one thing is
inconsistent with any other. With ideas, the opposite is the   10
case: in our ideas we join together and unite separate things,
which taken on their own are not inconsistent. This is the
origin of the contradiction.

[38]   Moreover, contradictoriness in our concepts arises merely
         from their obscurity and confusion: *there can be none in the case
         of clear and distinct ideas.*
                                                                [ibid.]

[O.] But why should there not be a contradiction in the
case of clear ideas which are inconsistent one with another.
Take, for example, the combination of the idea of a finite
being with that of an infinite being.

R. Even if those ideas are clear when taken apart, they are   5
certainly not clear when joined together. Your idea is thus
very obscure, for the conception you have of the combination and unity of the two ideas is not clear but extremely
obscure.

[39]   p. 445: When we examine through a magnifying glass those
        lines which appear straightest to us, we find them to be quite
        irregular, with undulating curves throughout. *And hence*, when
        in childhood we first saw a triangular figure drawn on paper,
        the figure could not have taught us how to conceive of a real
        triangle, as studied by geometricians.
                    [Fifth Replies: AT vii. 382; HR ii. 227]

[O.] But it is *from* the imperfect triangle that you frame in
your mind the perfect triangle.

[R.] But why then does the imperfect triangle provide me
me with the idea of a perfect triangle rather than an idea of
itself?   5

[O.] It provides you with both: firstly itself, and then,
from that, the perfect triangle. For you deduce the perfect
triangle from the imperfect.

[R.] That cannot be. I could not conceive of an imperfect
triangle unless there were in me the idea of a perfect one,   10
since the former is the negation of the latter. Thus, when I
see a triangle, I have a conception of a perfect triangle, and
it is by comparison with this that I subsequently realize that
what I am seeking is imperfect.

MEDIT. VI

[40]   p. 73: Further, I have the experience of making use of the
        faculty of imagination when I am occupied with those same
        material things; and from this it seems to follow that *they do
        exist*.
                    [AT vii. 71; HR i. 185]

That is, my body, which I make use of in the course of my
imagining.

[41]   p. 74: For *although I lacked it* [the power of imagination],
        I should none the less undoubtedly remain just the same
        individual as I now am.
                    [AT vii. 73; HR i. 186]

I should then be like the angels, who do not imagine.

[42]   If there exists some body to which my mind is so conjoined
that it can apply itself *to contemplate it, as it were,* whenever it
pleases, it is possible that by this very means I may imagine
corporeal things.

[ibid.]

[O.] What does 'to contemplate it' mean? Does it mean
the same as 'to understand it'? If so, why do you see a
different expression? If not, then the mind is more than an
understanding or thinking thing, and even before it has a
body it has this ability to contemplate a body. Or is this   5
ability of the mind an effect of its union with the body?

R. p.81: it is a special mode of thinking, which occurs as
follows. When external objects act on my senses, they print
on them an idea, or rather a figure, of themselves; and when
the mind attends to these images imprinted on the gland in   10
this way, it is said to *perceive.* When on the other hand the
images on the gland are not imprinted by external objects
but by the mind itself, which fashions and shapes them in
the brain in the absence of external objects, then we have
imagination. The difference between perception and imagina-   15
tion is thus really just this, that in perception the images are
imprinted by external objects which are actually present,
whilst in imagination the images are imprinted by the mind
without any external objects, and with the windows shut, as
it were. This makes it quite clear why I can imagine a   20
triangle, pentagon, and suchlike, but not, for example, a
chiliagon. Since my mind can easily form and depict three
lines in the brain, it can easily go on to contemplate them,
and thus imagine a triangle, pentagon, etc. It cannot, however, trace out and form a thousand lines in the brain except 25
in a confused manner, and this is why it does not imagine a
chiliagon distinctly, but only in a confused manner. This
limitation is so great that it is only with the greatest
difficulty that we can imagine even a heptagon or an octagon.
The author, who is a fairly imaginative man and has trained   30
his mind in this field for some time, can imagine these
figures reasonably distinctly; but others lack this ability.
This now also makes it clear why we see the lines as if they
were present in front of us, and it further explains the
surprising mental concentration we need for imagining,   35
and for contemplating, the body in this way. All this is clear
from what has been said.

[43]   p. 80: *And first of all, since* I know that all things which I understand clearly and distinctly can be produced by God just as I
understand them, my ability to understand one thing clearly
and distinctly apart from another is enough to enable me to be
certain that the two are distinct.

[AT vii. 78; HR i. 190]

You cannot ask whether the mind is a substance or, instead,
a mode; nor can you say that it can be both these, since that
is a contradiction; if it is one, it is not the other. You can,
however, pose the following question: since thinking or
thought is an attribute, to what substance does it belong? To   5
corporeal substance? Or rather to incorporeal and spiritual
substance? The answer to this is clear. You have a clear
conception of corporeal substance, and you also have a clear
conception of thinking substance as distinct from, and
incompatible with, corporeal substance, just as corporeal   10
substance is incompatible with thinking substance. In view
of this, you would be going against your own powers of
reasoning in the most absurd fashion if you said the two were
one and the same substance. For you have a clear conception
of them as two substances which not only do not entail one   15
another but are actually incompatible.

[44]   p. 84: For nature teaches through the sensations of pain,
hunger, thirst, etc. that I am not only present in my body as a
sailor is present in a ship, but that I am *very closely joined and, as
it were, intermingled* with it.

[AT vii. 81; HR i. 192]

[O.] But how can this be, and how can the soul be affected
by the body and vice versa, when their natures are completely different?

R. This is very difficult to explain; but here our experience
is sufficient, since it is so clear on this point that it just
cannot be gainsaid. This is evident in the case of the feelings
and so on.

[45]   p. 94: And although the parchedness of the throat does not
          always proceed, as it usually does, from the fact that a drink is
          necessary to the health of the body, but sometimes comes from
          some quite opposite cause, as in the case of a man with dropsy,
          yet *it is much better* that it should mislead on this occasion than
          that it should always mislead when the body is in good health.
                                        [AT vii. 89; HR i. 198]

[O.] But if this is the way our senses are naturally constituted, why did God not make up for this defect by giving
the soul awareness of the errors of the senses, so that it
could be on its guard against them?

R. God made our body like a machine, and he wanted it   5
to function like a universal instrument which would always
operate in the same manner in accordance with its own
laws. Accordingly, when the body is in good health, it gives
the soul a correct awareness; but when it is ill, it still affects
the soul in accordance with its own laws, and the necessary   10
result of this is a state of awareness under which the soul
will be deceived. If the body did not induce this misleading
state it would not behave uniformly and in accordance with
its universal laws; and then there would be a defect in God's
constancy, since he would not be permitting the body to   15
behave uniformly, despite the existence of uniform laws
and modes of behaviour.

[46]   p. 480: But the term 'surface' is used in two ways by mathe-
          maticians: in the sense of a body whose length and breadth
          alone they are studying and which *is considered apart from any
          depth* even though the possession of some degree of depth is
          not ruled out; or, secondly, as a mere mode of body, when all
          depth is completely denied.
                                        [Sixth Replies: AT vii. 433; HR ii. 249]

The mathematicians conceive of a surface as consisting of
many lines without depth, just as we call these boards, for
example, flat, when we do not see any depth in them.

[47]   p. 481: But I did not deny that it [the surface] was the extremity
        of a body. On the contrary, it can quite properly be called the
        extremity of the contained body, as much as of the containing
        one, in the sense in which bodies are said to be contiguous
        when their extremities are together.

                                                                    [ibid.]

[O.] This way of putting it is not in accordance with the
truth of the matter, for there is in fact only one extremity,
common to both bodies: when, in the Schools, two bodies
are said to be contiguous when their extremities are together, this is merely in accordance with the ordinary way   5
of talking. If, then, the extremities are together, or rather, as
we put it, if there is one extremity belonging to each body,
are the bodies contiguous or continuous? They seem to be
continuous, since the fact that two bodies have an identical
extremity seems quite sufficient for continuity. But if they   1c
are continuous, what are contiguous bodies going to be like?
Are they those which have a third body in between them?
But this is not what they are like.
    R. It is immaterial to me how other people define these
things. *I* call two bodies continuous when their surfaces are   1;
joined so immediately that when they move it is in a single
motion, and they both stop moving together. Bodies which
do not behave like this are contiguous.

[48]

A point to note is that you should not devote so much effort
to the *Meditations* and to metaphysical questions, or give
them elaborate treatment in commentaries and the like. Still
less should one do what some try to do, and dig more deeply
into these questions than the author did: he has dealt with
them quite deeply enough. It is sufficient to have grasped
them once in a general way, and then to remember the
conclusion. Otherwise, they draw the mind too far away
from physical and observable things, and make it unfit to
study them. Yet it is just these physical studies that it is most ·
desirable for men to pursue, since they would yield abundant
benefits for life. The author did follow up metaphysical
questions fairly thoroughly in the *Meditations,* and established

their certainty against the Sceptics and so on; so that everyone does not have to tackle the job for himself, or need to   15
spend time and trouble meditating on these things. It is
sufficient to know the first book of the *Principles*, since this
includes those parts of Metaphysics which need to be
known for Physics and so on.

[*Notes against a Programme*]

[49]

[O.] In the *Notes against a Programme*, p. 42, the author
says that no ideas of things, in the form in which we think
of them, are provided by the senses, but that they are all
innate. Does it then follow that the mystery of the Trinity,
for example, is innate?   5
R. The author does not say that all ideas are innate in
him. He says there are also some which are adventitious, for
example the idea he has of the town of Leyden or Alkmaar.
Secondly, even though the idea of the Trinity is not innate
in us to the extent of giving us an express representation of 10
the Trinity, none the less the elements and rudiments of the
idea are innate in us, as we have an innate idea of God, the
number three, and so on. It is from these rudiments, supplemented by revelation from the Scriptures, that we easily
form a full idea of the mystery of the Trinity. This how the 15
the conception we have of it is formed.

Principles of Philosophy

BK. I

[50]   Art. 23: And we must not think that God understands and
wills as we do, by means of operations that are in a certain way
distinct one from another; but rather that there is always a
single identical and perfectly simple act *by means of which* he
simultaneously understands, wills, and brings about all things.
                                              [AT viii. 14; HR i. 228]

We cannot conceive of how this happens, only understand it.
Any different conception we may have arises from the fact
that we think of God as a man who accomplishes all things

as we would—by means of many different acts. If, however, we pay careful attention to the nature of God, we shall see that we can only understand him as accomplishing all things by means of a single act.

[O.] It seems that this cannot be, since there are some of God's decrees which we can conceive of as not having been enacted and as alterable. These decrees, then, do not come about by means of the single act which is identical with God, since they can be separated from him, or at least could have been. One example of this, among others, is the decree concerning the creation of the world, with respect to which God was quite indifferent.

R. Whatever is in God is not in reality separate from God himself; rather it is identical with God himself. Concerning the decrees of God which have already been enacted, it is clear that God is unalterable with regard to these, and, from the metaphysical point of view, it is impossible to conceive of the matter otherwise.

Concerning ethics and religion, on the other hand, the opinion has prevailed that God can be altered, because of the prayers of mankind; for no one would have prayed to God if he knew, or had convinced himself, that God was unalterable. In order to remove this difficulty and reconcile the immutability of God with the prayers of men, we have to say that God is indeed quite unalterable, and that he has decreed from eternity either to grant me a particular request or not to grant it. Coupled with this decree, however, he has made a simultaneous decree that the granting of my request shall be in virtue of my prayers, and at a time when, in addition, I am leading an upright life; the effect of which is that I must pray and live uprightly if I wish to obtain anything from God. This then is the situation from the point of view of ethics; and here, after weighing the truth of the matter, the author finds himself in agreement with the Gomarists, rather than the Arminians or even, amongst his brethren, the Jesuits.

From the metaphysical point of view, however, it is quite unintelligible that God should be anything else but completely unalterable. It is irrelevant that the decrees could have been separated from God; indeed, this should not really be asserted. For although God is completely in-

different with respect to all things, he necessarily made the 45
decrees he did, since he necessarily willed what was best,
even though it was of his own will that he did what was best.
We should not make a separation here between the necessity
and the indifference that apply to God's decrees: although
his actions were completely indifferent, they were also com- 50
pletely necessary. Then again, although we may conceive
that the decrees could have been separated from God, this
is merely a token procedure of our own reasoning: the
distinction thus introduced between God himself and his
decrees is a mental not a real one. In reality the decrees could 55
not have been separated from God: he is not prior to them
or distinct from them, nor could he have existed without
them. So it is clear enough how God accomplishes all things
in a single act. But these matters are not to be grasped by our
powers of reasoning, and we must never allow ourselves the 60
indulgence of trying to subject the nature and operations of
God to our reasoning.

[51] Art. 26: For our part, in the case of anything for which, from
some point of view, we are unable to discover a limit, we shall
avoid asserting that it is infinite, and instead regard it as
indefinite.

[AT viii. 15; HR i. 230]

[*O.*] This distinction is the author's invention. But someone is going to say: 'What is the world like? Does it not have
set boundaries? Indeed, can anything exist as an actual individual entity without having a determinate nature and
boundaries? And does not the same apply to number, 5
quantity, and so on?'

R. As far as we are concerned, we are never able to discover a particular limit in these things, and so from our
point of view they are indefinite. What is more, they are
perhaps infinite, since when the indefinite is multiplied again 10
and again, as in this case, it is identical with infinity. So we
can perhaps say that the world is infinite, and the same for
number, etc. But as far as God is concerned, maybe he has a
conception and understanding of fixed limits in the world,
and in number, quantity, etc. He may be aware of some- 15
thing greater than the world, or number, and so on, and so

for him these things may be finite. As for us, we see that the nature of these things is beyond our powers, and realize that we cannot comprehend them since we are finite beings. Thus, from our point of view, they are indefinite or infinite. 20

[52] Art. 48: Whatever objects fall within the sphere of our knowledge I regard either as things, or affections of things, or *as eternal truths* which have no existence outside of our thought.

[AT viii. 22; HR i. 238]

[*O.*] But what becomes of contingent truths, like 'the dog is running' and so on?

R. By 'eternal truths' the author here means what are called common notions, such as 'it is impossible for the same thing to be and not to be', and so on. As for con- 5 tingent truths, these relate to existing things. Contingent truths involve existing things, and vice versa.

BK. II

[53] Art. 1: For we have a clear understanding of matter as a thing which is quite different from God and from ourselves or our mind; *and we appear to see clearly* that the idea of it comes to us from objects which are located outside of us, which it completely resembles.

[AT viii. 41; HR i. 254]

[*O.*] But why 'we *appear* to see'—an indication of doubt?

R. The reason I used that word is that perhaps anyone is capable of denying that we see the point in question. But in any case, what 'appears' to us is enough to prove what I want. For since we need to rely on our own minds and 5 what we are aware of in ourselves, what we 'see' must ultimately reduce to what 'appears' to us. And what appears to us in fact requires the existence of material objects as a source of the ideas in question.

[54]   Art. 26: We do not use any more force to move a stationary
        ship in calm water than we use to stop it suddenly when it is
        moving; or rather we use only slightly more: for one must
        subtract *the weight of the water displaced by the ship, and the
        viscosity of the water*, both of which could gradually bring it to a
        halt.

                                                  [AT viii. 55; AG 210]

This is something we see whenever a ship is sailing: water is
displaced by the sides of the ship and piles up higher than
the surrounding water. It stays piled up like this owing to
its weight; so the water would be capable of halting the ship
were it not driven on. What is meant by 'viscosity' is fairly
widely known.

[55]   Art. 32: We may distinguish two different motions in a
        carriage wheel—a circular motion about the axle, and a motion
        straight forward along the line of the road. But that these are
        not in reality distinct is clear from the following: every single
        point on the moving object describes only one single line. It
        does not matter that the line *is often very twisted*, so that it seems
        to be produced by many different sorts of motion; for we can
        imagine any line at all—even a straight line, the simplest of all
        —as the product of an infinite number of different motions.

                                                  [AT viii. 58; AG 212]

It is of course very twisted, since all the time it is moving on
through a large number of circles, as the wheel moves about
its axle. And the circles are not simple and perfect, but joined
up and twisted in a continuous forward motion. This
explains what I go on to say at the end of the section.   5

[56]   Art. 46: *The first rule* [for determining how much the motion
        of a body is altered by collision with other bodies].
                                                     [AT viii. 68]

Since many were complaining of the obscurity of these laws,
the author supplied a little clarification and further explanation in the French edition of the *Principles*.

BK. III

[57]   Art. 2: But it would be the height of presumption if we were
to suppose that all things were created by God *for our benefit
alone.*
[AT viii. 81; HR i. 271]

None the less, it is a common habit of men to suppose they
themselves are the dearest of God's creatures, and that all
things are therefore made for their benefit. They think their
own dwelling place, the earth, is of supreme importance,
that it contains everything that exists, and that for its sake   5
everything was created. But what do we know of what God
may have created outside the earth, on the stars and so on?
How do we know that he has not placed on the stars other
species of creature, other lives, and other 'men'—or at least
beings analogous to men? Maybe souls separated from   10
bodies, or other creatures whose nature escapes us are able
to live there. And how do we know that God has not produced an infinite number of kinds of creatures, and thus, as
it were, poured forth his power in the creation of things. All
these matters are surely quite hidden from us, since God's   15
purposes are hidden from us; and this is why we ought not
to have so high an opinion of ourselves as to think that
everything in the universe is to be found here on earth, or
exists for our benefit. For an infinite number of other
creatures far superior to us may exist elsewhere.   20

[58]   Art. 45: For there is no doubt that the world was *created* from
the very first *with every perfection that it now has.*
[AT viii. 99; AG 224]

The author could give an adequate explanation of the creation of the world based on his philosophical system, without
departing from the description in Genesis. (Incidentally, if
anyone can provide an explanation of this book the author
will regard him as a 'mighty Apollo', and the same goes for   5
the Song of Solomon and the Revelation.) The author did
at one time attempt such an explanation of the creation, but
he abandoned the task because he preferred to leave it to the
theologians rather than provide the explanation himself. As
far as Genesis is concerned, however, the story of the   10

creation to be found there is perhaps metaphorical, and so
ought to be left to the theologians. In that case, the creation
should not be taken as divided into six days, but the division
into days should be taken as intended purely for the sake of
our way of conceiving of things; this was the way Augustine   15
proceeded when he made the divisions by means of the
thoughts of the angels. Why, for example, is the darkness
said to precede the light? With regard to the waters of the
flood, they were undoubtedly supernatural and miraculous.
The statement about the cataracts of the deep is meta-   20
phorical, but the metaphor eludes us. Some say they came
down from heaven, and argue that this was where the waters
were originally placed at the creation, on the grounds that
God is said to have placed the waters above *ha shamayim*. But
this word is also very commonly used in Hebrew to denote   25
the air, and I think that it is out of a prejudice of ours that
we regard this as 'heaven'. Accordingly, the waters placed
above the air are clouds. There is another word in Hebrew
to denote the air, namely *ha aretz*.

[59]   Art. 46: From what has already been said we have established
         that the bodies which make up the universe are all composed
         of one and the same material, which is divisible in indefinitely
         many ways and is in actual fact divided into a large number of
         parts; these parts move in different directions *and have a sort of
         circular motion.*
                                         [AT viii. 100; AG 225]

[O.] But where was this assumed or proved?
R. In Book Two, where the author showed that all motion
was in some way circular.

[60]   So, if we may, we will suppose that the material of which the
         visible world is composed was originally divided by God into
         particles which were as nearly equal as possible, and *of a size
         which was moderate*, or intermediate when compared with those
         which now make up the heavens and stars.
                                    [ibid.: AT viii. 101; AG 225]

He calls them 'moderate' by comparison with the first
element; although they are too small, by a factor of one

hundred or more, to be detected by our senses. He uses the word 'intermediate' because they occupy an intermediate position between the first and third element.   5

[61]   These particles taken together possessed the same quantity of motion as is now found in the universe; and their motions were of two kinds, each of equal force: first, they moved individually and separately about their own centres, so as to form a fluid body such as I take the heavens to be; and in addition they moved together in groups *around certain other points* . . . so as to make up as many different vortices as there are now stars in the universe.

[ibid.]

[O.] But this hypothesis, which seems rather complicated, is simple enough, and Regius appears to have deduced it all from motion.

R. It certainly is simple enough—indeed it is extremely simple, if we consider the infinite number of consequences   5 deduced from it. A fluid body, which is what all this material is, moving in various different vortices: what simpler idea can there be, since it is the nature of a fluid body to move in and through vortexes? As far as Regius is concerned, however, his proof is worthless. What is surprising   10 is that in physics he has always been anxious to follow the views of the author and guess at them, even when he did not know them, whereas in metaphysics he has done everything possible to contradict the author's views, so far as his knowledge has allowed. However, this hypothesis of the   15 author is very simple, if we consider the almost infinite number of things he has deduced from it; and the deductive chain confirms the hypothesis. For the author subsequently saw that he could deduce practically everything from it. And he is willing to swear before God that when he was putting   20 forward these hypotheses he had not yet thought about fire, magnetism, and the rest; it was only afterwards that he saw that these things could be explained quite beautifully in terms of the original hypotheses. Indeed, in the *Treatise on the Animal*, which he worked on this winter, he noticed the   25 following: although his aim was merely to explain the functions of the animal, he saw that he could hardly do this

without having to explain the formation of the animal right
from the beginning. And this was something that he found
to be derivable from his principles, to the extent that he was   30
able to give a reason for the existence of the eye, nose, brain,
and so on. He clearly saw, moreover, that the nature of
things was so constituted in accordance with his principles
that it could not be otherwise. But these were all matters
which he did not wish to go into at such length and so he   35
gave up writing the treatise. However he confesses that the
few thoughts that he had concerning the universe are a
source of the greatest pleasure for him to look back on. He
values them most highly, and would not wish to exchange
them for any other thoughts he has had about any other   40
topic.

[62]   Art. 50: It must be noted that the smaller these fragments of
            other particles are, the more easily they move and can be
            reduced to other even smaller fragments. The reason is that
            the smaller they get, the greater the surface-area which they have
            in proportion to their mass; and the number of other bodies
            they come up against is a function of the surface-area, whereas
            the extent to which they split up is a function of their mass.
                                                          [AT viii. 104]

This is a matter of mathematics. But it must be taken to
apply to bodies having the same shape, for example two
spheres; otherwise the ratio does not hold. See p. 160.

[63]   *the greater surface-area they have*

                                                               [ibid.]

This is clear from the way a cube, for example, divides. If we
take a cube, which is made up of six sides, and divide it into
four parts, we shall have many more surfaces; and many
more still if the process is carried further with each of the
four parts.   5

[64]   *the extent to which they split up is a function of their mass.*
                                                               [ibid.]

The surface should not be excluded here, since the mass is
not separate from it, nor is it separate from the mass; but

here it is merely the theoretical notion of each of the two that we are introducing.

[65] Art. 53: We will not go wrong if we take all the material included in the space *AEI* and revolving round the centre *S* as the first heaven; and all that which makes up the innumerable other vortices revolving round the centres *F*, *f*, etc., as the second heaven; and lastly, whatever is found beyond these two heavens *as the third heaven*.

[AT viii. 106–7]

The author takes this third heaven to be the empyrean heaven, and he has argued that by comparison with the second heaven, let alone our own, it is immeasurably large. The fact that we think of our own heaven and earth as so large, and as containing all things, is due to prejudice. We 5 think of the earth as the end of all things, and do not consider that it too is a planet which moves like Mars, Saturn, etc.—bodies we do not make so much of. Yet before the creation of this universe and of space, there was nothing, neither space nor anything else. But God existed, im- 10 measurable and omnipresent, just as he is now. He was in himself; yet after he created the world he could not but be present in it.

[66] Art. 63: And it must be noted besides that the force of light does not consist in the duration of some movement, *but merely in pressure*, or in the first effort towards movement, even though the movement itself does not perhaps ensue.

[AT viii. 115]

Pressure can happen without movement. For example, we can take a metal instrument, or a piece of wood or metal, and press it with our hands on either side in such a way that no motion is produced, since of course the pressure and resistance on both sides are equal. The same thing happens 5 in this case. Material of the second element is pressed against our eye; but since there is some resistance in the eye it exerts pressure in turn on the material. Thus there is pressure on each side, yet without any movement. Although people refuse to accept this explanation of the nature of light, in a 10 hundred and fifty years time they will see that it is a good one, and that it is correct.

[67] Art. 66: And here it must be noted that there will be considerable harmony in these motions if the ecliptics of the first three vortexes, i.e. the circles furthest from the poles, meet exactly on the point E where the pole of the fourth vortex is located.
[AT viii. 117–18]

It is scarcely possible to understand this figure without the help of eight or so little balls to demonstrate the movement. The author, despite the fact that he has accustomed his mind to imagining, was scarcely able to conceive of it without the balls. So others will find it much more difficult. For these things depend on mathematics and mechanics, and can be demonstrated better in a visual demonstration than they can in a verbal explanation.

[68] Art. 68: Moreover, the inexplicable variety that is apparent in the way in which the fixed stars are located seems to make it quite clear that the vortexes which revolve round them *are not equal* in size.
[AT viii. 119]

[O.] But perhaps they are equal, and only seem unequal because of the unequal distance between them.
R. Well, that very fact would make them unequal in size. For the unequal distance between stars depends on the lack of equality in the vortexes which surround them, and the vortexes are therefore unequal in size.

[69] Art. 83: . . . and then also because it must be *narrower in the region of the centre* of any one of the neighbouring vortexes than in the region of its other parts: for all these reasons it is necessary that sometimes some of the globules move faster than others, since they must obviously change their order so as to move from a broader to a narrower passage.
[AT viii. 138]

As is clear from the figure on p. 78, the material contained between S and the centre F of the neighbouring vortex is

constricted in a more narrow space than that contained between *S*, *E*, and *F*. This is because the material in the former
case is constricted and compressed by *S* and *F*, which are   5
mutually adjacent; whereas in the latter case there is no such
compression from *S*, *E*, and *F*, because the space there is
free, and there is nothing to constrict or compress the
material.

[70] Art. 144: *Just as we see a top*, by the mere fact of being given one
      twist by a child, acquire enough force to keep on moving for
      several minutes and complete several thousand rotations in this
      time, despite the fact that its mass is very small and its motion
      is being impeded by the air that surrounds it and also the earth
      it rests upon; just so it is easy to believe that a planet, by the
      mere fact that it was in motion when it was first created, could
      have carried on making its circuits right up to the present
      time, without any notable reduction in speed.

                                                    [AT viii. 194]

This comparison is clear enough. The top would always
continue in its motion, were it not impeded by the air
around it; though, because it is small, it only resists the air
for a short time, viz. a few minutes; and in the same way the
stars would always continue in their motion, were they not   5
impeded by neighbouring bodies. However, since they are
very large bodies they resist the air that surrounds them and
other bodies all the more easily, and for several thousand
years at that. This is because the larger a body is, the more
easily it continues its motion and resists other bodies. And   10
the author can testify that he has seen a child's top of rather
large size carry on moving for nearly a quarter of an hour.
And this was just because of its large size. So it is with the
stars also. As to the top's having to resist the air, this is clear
from the fact that when you get nearer to the top you notice   15
a wind, which is produced by the resistance of the top and
the motion which it sets up in the air.

[71]   Art. 150: However, there are other causes besides this for the
         earth's rotation about its own axis. If it was previously a bright
         star occupying the centre of some vortex, then it undoubtedly
         had this sort of spinning motion; and now, the material of the
         first element, which has been collected together in the centre
         of the earth, still retains a similar motion and *so drives the earth.*
                                                              [AT viii. 198]

That is from within, of course, in so far as it moves it by
acting on its sides, in the same way as we see wind inflating a
bladder by moving its sides as soon as it is blown into it.

BK. IV

[72]   Art. 23: Now, all the space around the earth is occupied either
         by particles of terrestrial bodies, or by celestial matter. All the
         globules of the celestial matter have an equal tendency to move
         towards each other and away from the earth, and thus no in-
         dividual one has the force to displace any other. But the par-
         ticles of terrestrial bodies *do not have this tendency to so great an
         extent*; so whenever any celestial globules have any terrestrial
         particles above them, they must exert all their force to displace
         them. So the gravity of any terrestrial body is not really pro-
         duced by all the celestial matter surrounding it, but only and
         exactly by that part of it which rises into the space left by
         the body as it descends.
                                                              [AT viii. 213]

[O.] But the more solid a body is, the greater its centrifugal
force, as we can see in the case of a stone of a sling, which
moves faster than a piece of wood. Now the terrestrial
bodies are more solid, so . . .
R. I turn your own point against you. For in fact the   5
terrestrial bodies are not more solid than the celestial
globules; the opposite is true—or at least the two are equally
solid—and so the celestial globules move faster. Secondly,
the globules move far faster than the terrestrial bodies, since
they are smaller. And the earth itself is a large body full of   10
cavities and pores, which means that it easily loses its
motion and passes it on to another body. Thus, it cannot
move as fast as the globules; and so the globules, moving
faster than the terrestrial bodies, push them down and
make them heavy.   15

[73]   Art. 27: Next we should note that, although the particles of celestial matter move in many different ways at the same time, none the less the total overall effect of their individual opposition one to another is what amounts to *a state of equilibrium*.

[AT viii. 216]

In this way the entire system is in a state of equilibrium. But this is a very difficult thing to conceive of, because it is a mathematical and mechanical truth. We are not sufficiently accustomed to thinking of machines, and this has been the source of nearly all error in philosophy. You can observe the   5
total over-all effect I speak of in the case of wind or air when it is blown into a bladder. The total effect is to fill the bladder and produce movements in it; thus the air is in what amounts to a state of equilibrium, even though the particles that make it up move agitatedly in various different ways.   10

[74]   Art. 33: The shapes of the particles of the third element... are very various, and ... we may here distinguish the particles themselves *into three principal kinds*.

[AT viii. 220]

[O.] But how do we arrive at these three kinds?
R. Through reasoning, and then through experience, which confirms the reasoning. For we see that all terrestrial bodies are made up of the shapes in question: water is made up of oblong shapes, oil of branching shapes, and so on.

[75]   Art. 125: It is to be noted [concerning the formation of glass] that, when two bodies with extended surfaces meet each other directly face on, they cannot get so near to each other, since there is a space in between which is occupied by globules of the second element; but when one is *driven*, or slides, *on top of the other at an oblique angle*, they can join together much more closely.

[AT viii. 270]

[O.] But then they will still meet each other directly face on, except that this will merely be along a different side. And how is it that two bodies at rest against each other should stick together so firmly, when either one can easily move and thus be separated from the other?
R. When they are driven together directly face on, the

globules of the second element which are trapped between them are not expelled. When they come together obliquely, hither and thither, in this shape, Σ, they can expel the globules and join up and make one continuous body. This is how glass moves at first when it is hot—hither and thither at high speed; it moves more slowly when it begins to cool, and then finally comes to rest when it is cold. But it is impossible to conceive of what makes a body continuous and immobile, except its being in a state of rest.

[O.] But I could easily move such small particles with my hand, though I see they are now immobile.

R. If you could do this, the movements of your hand would be enough to destroy their state of rest, and so they would not be immobile. But in fact this is impossible, since the part of your hand which touches the parts of the hard body is softer than they are, and is thus unable to move them. The reasons for all this were explained quite adequately in Book Two. The nature of glass, which is otherwise so difficult to explain, is very easily accounted for on the basis of these principles.

From the *Discourse on the Method*

[76]   p. 1: Nothing is more equally distributed amongst men than good sense: for everyone *thinks he is abundantly provided* with it; so much so that even those whose desires are hardest to fulfil, and who are dissatisfied with all their other natural endowments, do not generally wish for a greater degree of good sense than they already possess.

[Part I: AT vi. 540 (1–2); HR i. 81]

[O.] But there are many obtuse men who frequently wish they had better and quicker minds.

R. I agree; there are indeed many who acknowledge themselves to be inferior to others in intelligence, memory, and so on. But none the less, everyone thinks that he is so excellent as to be second to none, when it comes to judgement, and being qualified to give an opinion. Everyone is happy with his own opinions, and no two people think alike. This is what the author means by 'good sense' in this passage.

[77]   p. 15: But on closer examination, I observed, *with regard to Logic,* that the forms of syllogism, and almost all the other rules, are of less use for exploring the gaps in our knowledge than for explaining to others what we already know, or, like the art of Lully, for prattling copiously and without judgement on matters we are ignorant of.

[Part II: AT vi. 549 (17); HR i. 91]

This really applies not so much to Logic, which provides demonstrative proofs on all subjects, but to Dialectic, which teaches us how to hold forth on all subjects. In this way it undermines good sense, rather than building on it. For in diverting our attention and making us digress into the stock   5 arguments and headings, which are irrelevant to the thing under discussion, it diverts us from the actual nature of the thing itself. Professor Voetius is a past master at this: throughout his books he simply presents his opinions, lays down the law—declaring 'this is how it is'—and then lumps   10 together a lot of authorities.

[78]   p. 17: The long chains of reasoning, made up of very simple and easy steps, which are used by Geometers to prove the most difficult theorems, gave me the idea that all the items which fall in the province of human knowledge might be *mutually related in the same sort of sequence.*

[Part II: AT vi. 550 (19); HR i. 92]

[O.] But is it not the case that in Theology too all the items are mutually related in the same sort of sequence and chain of reasoning?

R. Undoubtedly they are. But these are truths which depend on revelation, and so we cannot follow or under-   5 stand their mutual connection in the same way. And certainly Theology must not be subjected to our human reasoning, which we use for Mathematics and for other truths, since it is something we cannot fully grasp; and the simpler we keep it, the better Theology we shall have. If the   10 author thought anyone would abuse his Philosophy by taking arguments from it and applying them to Theology, he would regret all the trouble he had taken. However, we can and should prove that the truths of Theology are not inconsistent with those of Philosophy, but we must not in   1

any way subject them to critical examination. This is how the
monks have opened the way to all the sects and heresies—I
mean, through Scholastic Theology, which is something
that should above all else have been stamped out. Why do
we need to spend all this effort on Theology, when we see   20
that simple country folk have just as much chance as we have
of getting to heaven? This should certainly be a warning to
us that it is much more satisfactory to have a Theology as
simple as that of country folk than one which is plagued
with countless controversies. This is how we corrupt   25
Theology and open the way for disputes, quarrels, wars and
such like. Indeed, the theologians have made such a habit of
foisting every kind of doctrine on to the theologians of the
opposing school and then denigrating it, that they have
completed mastered the art of denigration, and can scarcely 30
do anything else but denigrate, even when they do not
mean to.

[79]   I knew that I should start with an examination of those items
        which were the simplest and easiest to grasp. And since I saw
        that, of all those who had sought the truth up to the present
        day, it was the mathematicians alone who had been able to dis-
        cover a number of demonstrative proofs (i.e. certain and
        evident reasons), I had no doubt that the object of their
        inquiries was the easiest of all. So I knew I should examine this
        first, even though the only benefit which I expected to ensue
        was that *my mind would gradually become used to recognizing the
        truth*, and to withholding assent from false reasoning.
                                                        [ibid.]

This benefit cannot be derived from Mathematics as it is
commonly taught. For this consists almost entirely in the
history or explanation of terms, and the like, all of which
can easily be learnt by memorization. All this develops the
memory, but not the intelligence. To enable the intelligence 5
to be developed, you need mathematical knowledge, and
this is something which is not to be gleaned from books,
but rather from actual practice and skill. The author had to
teach himself the subject this way, since he had no books
with him, and the results he obtained were very happy.   10
However, not everyone has this aptitude for Mathematics:
one needs a mathematical mind which must then be polished

by actual practice. Now this mathematical knowledge must
be acquired from Algebra; but this is a subject in which we
cannot do ourselves much good without the aid of a teacher 15
—unless, that is, we are willing to follow step by step the
lead which the author has given us in the *Geometry*, so as to
end up with the ability to solve problems and discover
truths whatever they may be, just as a certain Frenchman did
at Paris. 20

A study of Mathematics, then, is a prerequisite for making
new discoveries, both in Mathematics itself and in Philosophy. You do not, however, need Mathematics in order to
understand the author's philosophical writings, with the
possible exception of a few mathematical points in the 25
Dioptrics. The topics on which the author wants us to exercise our minds are very simple ones, such as the nature and
properties of the triangle and so on; these must be thought
about and pondered on. Mathematics accustoms the mind to
recognizing the truth, because it is in Mathematics that 30
examples of correct reasoning, which you will find nowhere
else, are to be found. Accordingly, the man who has once
accustomed his mind to mathematical reasoning will have a
mind that is well equipped for the investigation of other
truths, since reasoning is exactly the same in every subject. 35
The fact that there are some people who are clever at Mathematics but less successful in subjects like Physics, is not due
to any defect in their powers of reasoning, but is the result
of their having done Mathematics not by reasoning but by
imagining—everything they have accomplished has been by 40
means of imagination. Now, in Physics there is no place for
imagination, and this explains their signal lack of success in
the subject.

Then again, Mathematics accustoms the mind to distinguishing arguments which are true and valid from those 45
which are probable and false. For, in Mathematics, anyone
who relies solely on probable arguments will be misled and
driven to absurd conclusions; this will make him see that a
demonstrative proof does not proceed from probable premisses, which in this respect are equivalent to false ones, but 50
only from those which are certain. It is because philosophers
have not followed this advice that they can never distinguish
proofs from probable arguments in Philosophy and

Physics; moreover, they nearly always try to argue in terms
of probabilities, since they do not believe that there can be a   55
place for demonstrative proofs in the sciences which deal
with reality. And this is why the Sceptics and others have
believed that the existence of God cannot be proved, and
why many still think that it is unprovable; whereas in fact it
is conclusively provable and, like all metaphysical truths, is   60
capable of a more solid proof than the proofs of Mathematics. For if you were to go to the mathematicians and cast
doubt on all the things the author cast doubt on in his metaphysical enquiries, then absolutely no mathematical proof
could be given with certainty; whereas the author went on to   65
give metaphysical proofs in spite of the doubt. So the proofs
in Metaphysics are more certain than those in Mathematics.
And at every point, the author tried to provide 'mathematical' proofs, as they are commonly called, in his
philosophy; though these cannot be grasped as such by those   70
who are unfamiliar with Mathematics.

[80]   p. 20: Thus, in order that I should not remain irresolute in
       my actions while reason advised me to be so in my judgements,
       and so that I should start to live from that time on as happily
       as possible, I made up for myself a temporary code of ethics,
       consisting merely of three or four rules, which *I should like to
       include here.*
                          [Part III: AT vi. 552(22); HR i. 95]

The author does not like writing on ethics, but he was compelled to include these rules because of people like the
Schoolmen; otherwise, they would have said that he was a
man without any religion or faith and that he intended to
use his method to subvert them.   5

[81]   p. 36: *But if we did not know* that whatever reality and truth there
       is in us proceeds entirely from a supreme and infinite being,
       then no matter how clear and distinct our ideas were, we
       should have no reason for being certain that they were there-
       fore true.
                          [Part IV: AT vi. 562(39); HR i. 105]

If we did not know that all truth has its origin in God, then
however clear our ideas were, we would not know that they

were true, or that we were not mistaken—I mean of course when we were not paying attention to them, and when we merely remembered that we had clearly and distinctly perceived them. For on other occasions, when we do pay attention to the truths themselves, even though we may not know God exists, we cannot be in any doubt about them. Otherwise, we could not prove that God exists.

[82]   p. 56: It is true that there is nothing in the medicine which is currently practised of any remarkable utility. But, without having any intention of condemning it, I am confident that anyone, even a professional doctor, would agree that all the discoveries up to the present day are virtually nothing by comparison with what still remains to be known; and that men could achieve immunity from an infinite number of illnesses, both of the body and of the mind, and even *perhaps from the feebleness of old age*, if they only had a sufficiently extensive knowledge of the original causes of these maladies, and of all the remedies which nature has provided us with.
[Part VI: AT vi. 575(62); HR i. 120]

Whether man was immortal before the Fall, and if so how, is not a question for the philosopher, but must be left to the theologians. And as to how men before the Flood could achieve such an advanced age, this is something which defeats the philosopher; and it may be that God brought this about miraculously, by means of supernatural causes, and without recourse to physical causes. Or then again, it could have been that the structure of the natural world was different before the Flood, and that it then deteriorated as a result of the Flood. The philosopher studies nature, as he does man, simply as it is now; he does not investigate its causes at any more profound level, since this is beyond him. However, it should not be doubted that human life could be prolonged, if we knew the appropriate art. For since our knowledge of the appropriate art enables us to increase and prolong the life of plants and such like, why should it not be the same with man? But the best way of prolonging life, and the best method of keeping to a healthy diet, is to live and eat like animals, i.e. eat as much as we enjoy and relish, but no more.

[O.] This might work out all right in sound and healthy

bodies, where the appetite is working properly for the benefit of the body; but it will not work for those who are sick.

[R.] Nonsense. Even when we are ill nature still remains 25
the same. What is more, it seems that nature plunges us into illnesses, so that we can emerge all the stronger, and makes light of any obstacles in her way, provided we obey her. And perhaps if doctors would only allow people the food and drink they frequently desire when they are ill, they 30
would often be restored to health far more satisfactorily than they are by means of all those unpleasant medicines. Indeed, experience confirms this. In such cases nature herself works to effect her own recovery; with her perfect internal awareness of herself she knows better than the doctor who is 35
on the outside.

[O.] But there is such an infinite number of foods etc.; so what choice should we make among them, and what order should we take them in, and so on?

R. This is something our own experience teaches us. We 40
always know whether a food has agreed with us or not, and hence we can always learn for the future whether or not we should have the same food again, and whether we should eat it in the same way and in the same order. So, as Tiberius Caesar said (or Cato, I think), no one who has reached the 45
age of thirty should need a doctor, since at that age he is quite able to know himself through experience what is good or bad for him, and so be his own doctor.

Amsterdam, 20 April 1648.

CB 1–48. *Meditations* and *Replies to Objections*

This section deals with twenty-seven points from the *Meditations* and twenty from the *Replies*; the final passage (CB 48) is a general piece of advice on how to study the *Meditations*. The reader is referred to the Conspectus on pp. 121 ff. for a summary of the topics discussed.

The section is divided into six groups of pieces, headed 'Medit. I', 'Medit. II', etc. In each group, firstly passages from the appropriate Meditation are discussed, in the order in which they come in the original text; then Burman introduces various quotations from the *Replies* relevant to the Meditation under discussion. The only exception to this orderly procedure (except for the placing of CB 22 and 36—see Commentary ad loc.) occurs in the first group of pieces (CB 1–9). Here CB Nos. 1–3 indeed deal with the First Meditation; but Nos. 4–9 (from the *Replies*) concern issues more relevant to the subsequent Meditations (the Cogito, the Circle, the nature of the mind).

CB 1. ll. 1–3. From the senses . . . through the senses. Here, in the first paragraph, we have an example of the philosophical richness of the *Conversation*. The casual reader of the passage quoted from the First Meditation might suppose that Descartes was merely referring in a general way to the fact that our ordinary beliefs are based on the perceptions of the five senses. But Descartes makes it clear to Burman that the phrase *vel a sensibus vel per sensus* marks a specific distinction between two different sources of our beliefs. The distinction, as it is explained here, looks a bit like Russell's famous contrast between knowledge by acquaintance and knowledge by description. 'In the presence of my table', writes Russell, 'I am acquainted with . . . its colour, shape, . . . etc.' This is knowledge by acquaintance. On the other hand, when I know some piece of information about the world, e.g. that the Emperor of China exists (or did in 1912)—this is knowledge by description. (RUSSELL, p. 25.)

However, under knowledge by acquaintance Russell includes, for obvious reasons, the data of touch, taste, etc., as well as sight; and similarly, my knowledge by description can be acquired otherwise than by hearing (e.g. by reading a book). So, if Descartes has this kind of contrast in mind, why should he have fastened exclusively on the senses of sight and hearing to gloss *a sensibus* and *per sensus* respectively? Clauberg, in his commentary on this part of the *Meditations*, makes the same special reference to sight and hearing that we find here. Moreover, he implies that Descartes regarded sight as *par excellence* the sense of discovery (*inventionis sensus*): the eyes are the windows of the mind, through which all the various data of colour, shape, movement, etc., enter our consciousness. Similarly, hearing is *par excellence* the *sensus disciplinae*—the sense of learning. The other senses, says Clauberg, are passed over by Descartes because their contribution to our knowledge is by comparison negligible (since they only provide us with information about our immediate environment) (CLAUBERG, pp. 9–10).

If we accept Clauberg's account, and combine it with our parallel with the Russell distinction, then what Descartes is saying is this: what we have hitherto accepted as knowledge is of two kinds, viz. (1) acquaintance with sensory data (colours, shapes, etc.)—principally and typically through the sense of sight; and (2) descriptive knowledge (information about the external world, what exists and so forth)—principally and typically acquired through the 'sense of learning', hearing.

But there is still a problem with this interpretation. Whatever I have hitherto accepted as *most true*, says Descartes, I have acquired either from the senses or through the senses. Yet the sort of knowledge that is opposed to error is knowledge *that* something is the case; it is only knowledge by description that can properly speaking be called knowledge of truths (cf. RUSSELL, p. 23). Is it not then a confusion for Descartes to include knowledge by acquaintance (knowledge of colours, shapes, etc.) under the heading of 'what I have hitherto accepted as most true'? However, Descartes holds that even in this sphere there is, or can be, a residual judgemental element of a very special sort; so that there can, even here, be room for error. For this notion, see below on CB 15.

1. 7. common principles. These *principia communia* are referred to further down as 'common principles and axioms' (line 13). The example given at line 13 appears in the *Principles* (Bk. I, Art. 49), where it is also called a 'common notion' (*notio*); another example given is *ex nihilo nihil fit*. There is a list of ten such propositions, under the heading 'axioms or common notions' in the Second Replies (AT vii. 164–6; HR ii. 55).

1. 8. never in the senses (Med., p. 34): 'page 34' is AT vii. 39–40 (see Introduction, p. xiv); the reference is to Descartes' discussion of innate ideas in the Third Meditation, where God's existence is proved from the innate idea I have of God.

11. 8/10. I acquired these . . . through hearing. Descartes is not denying the innateness of the 'common principles'. His point is that unless we actually 'hear' them—i.e. are explicitly taught them by our logic tutor or whoever—we are not conscious of them at all (although they are implicitly presupposed by our ways of thinking about particulars; see lines 17/22 and CB 4).

l. 12. knows he is aware of (*scit se nosse*): an awkward phrase to translate; Adam has 'sait être en sa connaissance'. To render 'know he *knows*' would be misleading; for Descartes' man who is 'beginning to philosophize' is making a review of his hitherto accepted beliefs: these may or may not turn out to be cases of genuine knowledge.

l. 15. creatures of the senses. Reliance on the senses for Descartes, as for Plato (cf. *Republic*, 523 ff.), is the mark of the uncritical, 'prephilosophical' man. Descartes' description here of the way we think 'before we begin to philosophize' throws light on several important topics in the *Meditations*. See Introduction, pp. xxiv, xxxiii.

l. 27. here we are dealing primarily. This is a rather free version of the idiomatic Latin 'hic praecipue de re existente agitur, an ea sit'. The *hic* could be taken to refer to this particular part of the argument (the first stage of doubt). But I believe the point in fact applies to the First Meditation taken as a whole. The *Synopsis* supports this more general interpretation of the referent of *hic*: 'In prima [Meditatione] causae exponuntur propter quas de rebus omnibus, *praesertim materialibus*, possumus dubitare' (AT vii. 12; my italics). The implied continuation of Descartes' point must be: 'but of course the common principles are not relevant to this issue, since they do not assert anything about real existence in the world'. For this lack of existential import cf. *Principles* I, 10.

CB 2. l. 3. customary difficulties of the Sceptics. The old Pyrrhonian arguments about the reliability of the senses had been much discussed by the Sceptics of the sixteenth century (see POPKIN, Chs. II, III); and the dreaming argument, too, has a long ancestry (cf. Plato, *Theaetetus*, 158). Indeed, Hobbes had ribbed Descartes for bringing up 'that old stuff' (*vetera illa*: AT vii. 171). Although Descartes implies that his demon argument goes beyond these customary objections, he does not explain exactly in what respect this is so. (See FRANKFURT, p. 87, for one suggestion of a special additional role for the demon.)

l. 7. which some might criticize as a superfluous addition. This appears to be the sense of the curious clause in the MS.: 'quam sursum dari aliquis objicere potest'. Adam suggests emending *sursum* to *seorsum*, and translates 'qu'on peut lui objecter qu'il introduit hors de propos' (ADAM, ad loc.).

CB 3. l. 1: contradictory. For the contradiction, see below on CB 10.

CB 4. 1. 2. Before this inference. The text has 'ante hanc conclusionem', which two recent writers who have referred to this passage in the *Conversation* have translated as 'before this conclusion' (FRANKFURT, p. 97; KENNY (1), p. 51). But 'conclusion' seems inappropriate as a description of the entire phrase 'cogito ergo sum'; it would be normal in English to call *sum* the conclusion, and the phrase as a whole an argument or 'inference'. And in fact *conclusio* in Latin is quite capable of bearing this more appropriate meaning. (The *Oxford Latin Dictionary* gives 'the inferring or deducing of a proof' as the first meaning of *'conclusio'*. Compare also the meaning of *conclusion* in French.) *Concludere* is used to mean 'infer' at CB 17 and CB 19.

ll. 8/9. or that I know it before my inference. MS.: 'non ideo semper expresse et explicite cognosco illam praecedere et scio ante meam conclusionem'. I prefer to take *ante* as a preposition governing *conclusionem*, and *scio* as governed by the *non* at the beginning of the sentence with *illam* as the understood object. Adam, however, takes *ante* as adverbial and translates 'mais je ne sais pas pour cela expressément et explicitement qu'elle précède, et je connais ma conclusion auparavant'. But on either rendering the crucial point is the same, viz. that one can make the inference 'cogito ergo sum' without express and explicit awareness of the priority of the major premiss. (See Introduction p. xxiii ff.)

l. 12. As I have explained before: at CB 1, lines 17–22.

CB 5. This is one of the pieces which I have punctuated differently from Adam (see Introduction, p. xv). Adam gives the whole piece to Burman, except for the final reply on memory (lines 20–23). It seems to me more natural to make the first chunk (lines 1–12) a piece of straight commentary attributable to Descartes (the assertion at lines 7 ff. is particularly characteristic). If this is right, then it is only at line 13 that Burman breaks in with an objection. For this format, compare CB 22 and CB 50.

l. 4. cannot incline to nothingness. Descartes originally raised the question of God and deception in the First Meditation, and he takes it up again at the end of the Third Meditation. There he has some relatively straightforward arguments to prove that God cannot deceive: 'God is supremely perfect, but deception implies some defect (*defectum*)' (AT vii. 52, line 7); 'God is supremely good, but the will to deceive is a sign of malice (*malitia*)' (Fourth Meditation, *ad init.*: AT vii. 53, line 27). But the passage from the Sixth Replies quoted here by Burman refers to a rather more complex argument in the Fourth Meditation (AT vii. 54; HR i. 172). It is this which Descartes attempts to develop and clarify here at CB 5 (he refers to it at line 5 as a 'metaphysical consideration'; MS. 'et haec md. [=meditatio, Adam] metaphysica est'). The following steps seem to be involved:

(1) God is pure being;

(2) we human beings are a mixture of being and non-being;

(3) our error derives from that part of us which involves non-being;

(4) God cannot incline to non-being;

hence (5) God cannot deceive.

Propositions (1) and (2) seem to stem ultimately from neo-Platonic Christian theology: God (like Plato's forms) has 'pure being' because he possesses his attributes permanently and unchangeably; finite creatures are less real (have less 'being') because they possess their attributes less fully and permanently (cf. *Republic*, 477a; *Symposium*, 211a). But even if we grant Descartes his Platonic apparatus, the remaining steps seem highly dubious. Why should God not be responsible for error and imperfection? It does not help to be told that God cannot 'incline to nothingness' (*ferri in nihil*, line 4) or 'tend to non-being' (*tendere in non ens*, line 12), for we still want to know why being cannot be responsible for non-being. Descartes might have replied that the elements of non-being are mere 'negations' or the absence of features, rather than positive features requiring a cause. But he himself was not quite satisfied with classing error as simply a 'negation' (cf. AT vii. 55, line 1); moreover, the distinction between positive and negative predicates implied in such a defense is highly problematic (see commentary on CB 19).

l. 7. faculty of perception (*facultas percipiendi*). Descartes is referring to the *lumen naturale*—the faculty that enables us to 'intuit' or 'clearly and distinctly perceive' certain truths. Throughout this passage the threat of the 'Cartesian circle' looms in the background. If I use the faculty of perception correctly, by assenting only to what I clearly perceive, says Descartes, I cannot be deceived (lines 8/9). Why not? Evidently because the faculty is the gift of God (lines 7/8); compare line 16: 'a reliable mind was God's gift to me' (ingenium . . . a Deo rectum accepi). But if the reliability of the mind can be established only after God's existence has been proved, how do we manage to prove his existence in the first place? Compare CB 6.

ll. 9/10. cannot be deceived. There is a danger here of Descartes' argument proving too much. If it is (logically) impossible that we should be deceived by God, how is this to be reconciled with the undoubted fact that we do sometimes go astray? This difficulty is discussed in the Fourth Meditation, where Descartes offers two explanations of the fact that we are occasionally subject to error. The first is really a non-explanation: we just cannot understand the hidden purposes of God (AT vii. 55). The second has to do with the perfect and unlimited power of our will (see below on CB 31 line 20). In the Sixth Meditation, there is a third argument (see below on CB 45).

l. 17. but my memory may still deceive me. Compare *Principles* I, 44: 'A very frequent source of error is that there are many things which we think we have perceived in the past; these get stored in our memory and we give our assent to them, just as if we had actually perceived them, even though in fact we have never done so' (AT viii. 21). For Descartes' strikingly off-hand reply to Burman's objection (lines 20 ff.), see Introduction, p. xxvii.

CB 6. l. 2: uses axioms: for example 'tantumdem esse debet in causa efficiente et totali quantum in ejusdem causae effectu' ('There must be at least as much in the efficient and total cause as in the effect of that cause: AT vii. 40; HR i. 162). For the term 'axiom', which is not actually used in the Third Meditation (though it is in the Second Replies: AT vii. 165 ff.), see below on CB 52. The proof of God's existence referred to is the one which starts from the existence of an idea of God in the mind.

l. 10. our mind can think of only one thing at a time. It is essential to Descartes' rebuttal of the charge of circularity that the mind be able to focus on the premises which prove God's existence *all at once*. It is not enough to review them in turn; they must all be attended to together. For the certainty and guarantee of truth lasts *only as long as the attention* (ll. 7/8. MS.: quamdiu id facit (sc. attendit); see further Introduction, p. xxx). Burman, however, doubts whether the mind can really attend to all the relevant axioms at once; will not one thought impede the next (lines 14/16)? This is a serious and disturbing objection which Descartes never really answers satisfactorily. He does give a straightforward example, taken from his own immediate experience, to show that one can think of two things at once (lines 20/21). But the two thoughts offered are of absolutely minimal complexity; compare the propositions involved in proving God's existence, e.g. the one quoted in the note on line 2 above.

l. 12. every thought occurs instantaneously (*omnis cogitatio fit in instanti*). To rebut this thesis Descartes simply observes (lines 24/5) that one can continue thinking the same thing for some time. The rebuttal seems so elementary that one wonders how Burman can possibly have advanced the thesis in the first place. But it is possible that an ambiguity in the concept 'thought' (*cogitatio*) underlies what is apparently a simple empirical mistake. By a *cogitatio* one might mean the object of thought—that which is before the mind—i.e. an idea or proposition (cf. the Second Replies, where a *cogitatio* is defined as that *of which* we are aware: AT vii. 160). A *cogitatio* in this sense is not an event at all, but rather a timeless object; so it is at least conceivable that someone, focusing on the idea that *cogitationes* have no duration, might call them 'instantaneous'. Alternatively, however, one might use *cogitatio* to refer to the psychological act of thinking of something, i.e. some sort of mental process. This must be how Descartes takes it when he implies that *cogitatio* is an act (*actio*, line 24). A *cogitatio* in this sense must of course take up time; depending on the circumstances, it may be fleeting or protracted.

ll. 18/19. cannot think of a large number of things at the same time. In the margin of the original MS. at this point we find 'Conf. Dioptr., p. 148'. (The page reference is to the 1644 Latin edition of the *Discourse, Dioptric*, etc.; see Introduction, p. xiv.) The passage referred to (AT vi. 621) contains this strikingly relevant sentence: 'it is impossible for us to see distinctly more than one object at a time' (*fieri non posse ut amplius quam unum objectum simul distincte intueamur*). The purpose of the marginal note would thus seem to be to point out Descartes' view on the limitations of ordinary visual attention, and contrast it with the powers of mental attention he optimistically ascribes to us here in the *Conversation*. The note may perhaps represent an afterthought of Burman on how he might have presented his objections concerning the 'circle' more forcefully (see above on line 10).

ll. 27/28. thought will be extended and divisible. Burman's point, presumably, is that it is inconsistent with Descartes' own dualistic doctrines that thought, which belongs to the world of mind (*res cogitans*), should be characterized in terms which appear to place it in the world of matter (*res extensa*). One might expect Descartes to reply that there is a difference between temporal extension and spatial extension. And this is apparently what he does; though he expresses the distinction rather oddly as a distinction between something's being extended as to its duration, and *essentially* extended or extended as to its nature (lines 29–32; the term 'nature' is more or less interchangeable with 'essence' in Descartes; see below on CB 34). Thought can take time, Descartes admits, but that does not mean that it is extended substance: its duration, but not its 'nature', is extended and divisible.

This is all very well, but might not duration be relevant to essence? If my mind is a succession of different thoughts which are discrete occurrences occupying time like any other process, does this not, at least prima facie, cast doubt on the alleged indivisibility of my essence as a thinking being? Descartes attempts to clear this up by means of a comparison with the eternal nature of God, whose essence is indivisible even though his duration can be divided up (lines 33 ff.).

The problem with this is that God is something of a special case. We know *a priori*, as a truth of the natural light, that nothing can be added to or taken away from his nature (line 39; for additional difficulties in the parallel with God cf. the letter to Arnauld of 4 June 1648: AT v. 193). But since this is not so in the case of the human mind, what is to rule out the possibility of a radical interruption of the succession of thoughts; or what is to prevent a large portion of my mental life becoming 'detached' (e.g. by amnesia)? Descartes surely needs an independent argument to show that such an occurrence would not detract from my 'essential nature'. Yet this, so far as I know, he never offers. What is more, on Descartes' own argument in the Third Meditation, the logical possibility of fragmentation of mental life seems very much open: for without the conserving power of God, there would be nothing to guarantee my continued existence from one moment to the next (AT vii. 48–9). Descartes might have replied to this that a mind, even after such a traumatic occurrence, would still be a whole undivided mind. For 'we cannot conceive of half a mind, as we can conceive of half a body, however small' (*Synopsis*, AT vii. 13). But this is far from conclusive. For, it seems to me, the decision to call the traumatized mind a whole undivided mind is no less debatable than the original claim that the mind is indivisible.

l. 36. all at once and once for all (*simul et semel*). Though the general sense of this is clear (viz. that God's eternal being somehow transcends our ordinary temporal categories and so cannot be said to involve duration in any ordinary sense), the precise force of the two Latin terms in this context is hard to pin down. To begin with, the proposition *eternitas est simul* is logically odd. *Simul* is a two-place predicate: X and Y can be *simul* if they occur at the same time; but a single object can hardly be just 'simultaneous' *tout court*. Presumably the point is that there are no two distinct or separate times within eternity (i.e. if, *per impossibile*, one could speak of two separate occasions within eternity, they would necessarily count as simultaneous). *Aeternitas est semel* is equally difficult: perhaps the idea is that there is no *semel, bis, ter*—no 'once, twice, thrice'—involved in eternity, but only *semel*.

l. 47. could have done just the same before creation. As Descartes points out at CB 23, if we can accept the notion of a future eternity (belief in which is an article of the Christian faith), there should be no additional difficulty in the idea of a past eternity (lines 19 ff.; see commentary ad loc.).

CB 7. Burman attempts a *reductio ad absurdum* of the Cartesian doctrine of the 'perfect transparency of the mind', viz. the thesis that I am aware (*conscius*) of everything in my mind. (This thesis is stated explicitly in the quotation at CB 7, and is implicit in the argument of Meditation III, esp. AT iii. 49; HR i. 169.) Burman's attack fails because it depends on the premiss that the mind cannot have more than one thought at a time; as Descartes points out (line 10), this has already been disposed of (CB 6, lines 17 ff.).

A more promising version of Burman's objection had been canvassed by Hobbes in the form of an infinite regress argument: 'I do not realize that I am thinking by means of another thought (*cogitatio*); for although someone may think that he *was* thinking (which thought is just the same as remembering), it is quite impossible to think that one *is* thinking, or know one knows. For an infinite question would arise: "How do you know that you know that you know . . . ?" ' (Third Objections: AT vii. 173; HR ii. 62). Descartes' reply to this is very cavalier: 'It is irrelevant to say, as the philosopher does here, that one thought cannot be the subject of another thought. For who, apart from the objector himself, ever supposed that it could be?' (AT vii. 175; HR ii. 64). Unfortunately for Descartes, the answer to his rhetorical question is that he himself supposed that one thought could be the subject of another thought. This is made quite explicit when Descartes says to Burman here at CB 7 that to be aware is both to think and to reflect on one's thought (conscium esse est . . . cogitare et reflectere supra suam cogitationem: lines 7/8). Since Descartes elsewhere stipulates that everything in the mind *qua* thinking thing is a thought (see quotation at CB 8), the 'reflection' here has to be a *cogitatio* which has as its subject the original thought. (See further AT vii. 559; HR ii. 343, for Descartes' attempts to extricate himself from this difficulty.)

1. 10. soul is capable. I have followed the standard practice of translators of Descartes in rendering *anima* as 'soul' and *mens* as 'mind'. It should be borne in mind, however, that the two terms are more or less interchangeable in Descartes: *anima* (here) and *mens* (e.g. at CB 6, line 17) are both simply names for thinking substance (*res cogitans*). Cf. CB 9, lines 10 and 17.

CB 8. l. 1. For example, the movement of the arm. This is made a little clearer if we compare the passage from the Second Replies (AT vii. 160; HR ii. 53) where Descartes defines thought (*cogitatio*) as 'whatever is inside us in such a way that we are immediately aware of it'. He goes on to say: 'I have inserted "immediately" so as to exclude the consequences of thoughts; a voluntary movement, for example, certainly originates in a thought, but it is not itself a thought.' Descartes thus holds the view that, when I am aware of raising my arm, it is only the mental component (presumably the volition to raise my arm) that I am immediately aware of. The movement itself, though 'dependent on' a *cogitatio*, is not itself a *cogitatio*, and so is not an object of immediate awareness.

CB 9. l. 7: actual idea of God. Burman is still bothered by the Cartesian thesis that one is aware (*conscius*) of everything in one's mind (see above on CB 7). He argues here that the thesis sorts ill with Descartes' hypothesis of innate ideas. An innate idea (e.g. of God) is certainly a mental content, so it ought to follow, on Descartes' view, that the infant is aware of it. And if awareness is to mean anything at all, then the idea in question must be fully and completely present to the mind (*actualis*), not merely a potentiality. (See further Introduction, pp. xxxii ff.)

ll. 21/22. scarcely think of more than one thing. MS.: 'Sic homines semisomnolenti de nulla alia re vix cogitant.' Adam suggests emending the text here, but the pleonasm is probably good conversational Latin. What Descartes seems to mean is that when we are half asleep the mind is so 'swamped' with confused bodily stimuli that it loses the power to focus coherently on a number of thoughts at once.

l. 28. imprinted in the brain, like this. In the MS., there follows a curious squiggle which, as Adam notes, could have been intended as some kind of illustration of a brain trace, or, alternatively, may just be a crossing out by the copyist (AT v. 150). Some sort of illustration, however, seems more likely. See the letter to Meyssonier of 29 January 1640, where Descartes compares the 'impressions preserved in the memory' to 'folds which remain in the paper after it has once been folded' (AT iii. 20; K 70).

The idea of 'traces' or 'vestiges' physically present in the cerebrum has a rather modern ring to it; but it was a traditional scholastic doctrine that the seat of the 'sensible' or 'corporeal' memory was in the brain—more precisely the occipitium (GILSON (1), No. 276, p. 178); this is a fairly commonsense hypothesis to arrive at in view of phenomena like amnesia caused by a bang on the back of the head. Descartes, however, takes the view that the traces may be located throughout the brain, and in some cases even in parts of the rest of the body: 'for instance, the skill of a lute-player is not only in his head but partly in the muscles of his hands, and so on' (letter to Meyssonier already cited; cf. letter to Mersenne of 1 April 1640, AT iii. 48). Descartes denies the crude Aristotelian view that the physical traces are actual images or likenesses of what is remembered (cf. AT vi. 112–13; Aristotle, *De Mem.* 450a, 30 ff.).

l. 32. it cannot be without *some* thought. This is the orthodox Cartesian doctrine. Compare *Principles* I, 64: 'Thought and extension may be taken as modes of substance; that is, in so far as one and the same mind can have many different thoughts, and one and the same body, while retaining the same size, can be extended in various different ways.' Up to a point the parallel is clear. Just as a lump of stuff, e.g. the famous piece of wax, can take on various shapes, so that no one shape is essential to its being that particular lump of stuff (though having *some* shape or other is essential); in the same way, the mind can have many different thoughts, so that no one thought is essential to its being that particular mind (though *some* thought or other is essential). Cf. the letter to Arnauld written a few months after the *Conversation* (AT v. 221) and also the letter to Gilbieuf of 19 January 1642 (AT iii. 418; K 125).

ll. 36/7. intellectual memory. Aquinas distinguished between *memoria intellectiva*, whose job was to conserve general concepts or universals, and *memoria sensitiva* (possessed by animals as well as men), by means of which particular impressions are stored (*Cont. Gent.* II, 74; cf. GILSON (1), pp. 177–8). As we can see from this exchange with Burman, Descartes accepted both the distinction made by Aquinas and the role assigned by him to intellectual memory (viz. that of concept retention). Other passages from the correspondence make it clear that Descartes regards the intellectual memory as entirely independent of the body: 'je reconnais une autre [mémoire], du tout intellectuelle, qui ne dépend que de l'âme seule' (letter to Mersenne, AT iii. 48; K 72).

There are no doubt good doctrinal reasons for believing in a completely non-physical faculty of memory (survival of the personality after death, for instance, would hardly make sense without it). But the argument for the existence of intellectual memory which Descartes presents to Burman here is of quite a different kind. There is no relationship between the letters K–I–N–G and the meaning of the word (line 46); *ergo*, Descartes seems to argue, my ability to grasp the meaning when I hear the word must be due to intellectual memory. What Descartes means by 'relationship' (*affinitas*) is obscure. There is certainly a *conventional* relationship between 'king' and the concept *king*, viz. that of sign to *significatum*. Presumably, then, Descartes means that there is no *natural*, non-arbitrary relationship between the term and its meaning (in the way there is, perhaps, between the symbol ♀ and the idea of a man). But what is to prevent a connection being as it were artificially forged by a process of conditioning, so that the appearance or sound of the word 'king' becomes a stimulus to which we respond by coming up with the relevant idea? In fact Descartes himself, in a letter to Mersenne (18 March 1630; AT i. 134; K 8) talks of the fact that various sounds can 'evoke ideas in our mind'. He goes on: 'I think that if you thoroughly whipped a dog five or six times to the sound of the violin, he would begin to whine and run away as soon as he heard that music again.' The example is particularly awkward for Descartes' position here at CB 9; for there is certainly no *affinitas* between the sound of a violin and the idea of being whipped.

Descartes, however, has an answer to this criticism. He would have denied that the violin is, for the dog, genuinely the sign of an idea. This is made clear in the letter to Newcastle of 23 November 1646 (AT iv. 574; K 207):

If you teach a magpie to say good-day to its mistress when it sees her coming, all you can possibly have done is to make the emitting of this word the expression of one of its feelings. For instance, it will be an expression of the hope of eating, if you have habitually given it a titbit when it says the word. Similarly, all the things which dogs, horses, and monkeys are made to do are merely expressions of their fear, their hope, or their joy; and consequently they can do these things without any thought . . .

The topic here is, of course, the making rather than the recognition of signs. But the crucial point to emerge if we combine what is said in the letter with the remarks to Burman is this: Descartes holds that the use (production and recognition) of genuine signs is in an important sense 'stimulus-free', so that such understanding cannot be explained by a 'sensitive memory' shared by animals. By 'genuine' signs, I mean to convey that, as Descartes puts is, 'the signs must be relevant to the topic so as to exclude the speech of parrots' (to Newcastle, ibid.). Another important requirement (which is also demanded by the notion of 'intellectual memory'—see CB 9, line 50) is that the signs be universal: that is, the user must understand that a given sign refers indifferently to any member of the relevant class, irrespective of particularities of time and circumstance. (For further discussion of Descartes' views on language see CHOMSKY, Ch. I.)

CB 10. ll. 1/2: saying something contradictory. This repeats what was asserted at CB 3. But the proposition, 'there exists a supremely powerful and malignant being', is not, on the face of it, inconsistent. It is easy to see that supposing *God* to be malicious might involve inconsistency; but the malignant demon was apparently introduced precisely to avoid this (see quotation at CB 2). What is more, the escape clause, 'if it is permissible to say so' (si fas est dicere), suggests an attempt to avoid impiety rather than logical incoherence (compare the French version 'si je l'ose dire'). In fact, on the strength of this very passage, Descartes had been accused of blasphemy in maintaining that God was a deceiver (see letter to the Curators of Leyden University, 4 May 1647, AT v. 7–10; K 218).

None the less it is clear from our passage here at CB 10 that it was concern about the *logical* status of his supposition that was Descartes' principal reason for adding the restrictive clause. Apparently Descartes regarded the demon hypothesis as incoherent because *supreme* power implies perfection, and perfection is inconsistent with the will to deceive. Compare AT v. 8 (letter referred to already):

Since the context required me to make the supposition of some supremely powerful deceiver, I make the distinction between the good God and the evil demon; and I said that if *per impossibile* there were such a supremely powerful deceiver, he would still not be the good God, since he *would have the defect entailed by deceitfulness* (deceptio), but could only be regarded as some malignant demon. [italics mine]

CB 11. ll. 1/2. But is it God. I follow the MS.: 'Sed an Deus? Non, nescio, potius genius ille qui me deludit, qui me etiam creavit.' Adam prefers to emend the text here, but the original just about makes sense if we understand *est* in front of *genius* (though the isolated *nescio* is rather harsh). The general sense, in any case, is not in doubt.

CB 12 and 13. These pieces are discussed in the commentary on CB 22, q.v.

CB 14. Adequate knowledge. In the Fourth Replies, Descartes asserted that one could never know one had adequate knowledge; if one could, one's knowledge would have to equal God's. Burman, as his question shows, had missed the point of the reference to God. The point has nothing to do with theology, but is simply a *reductio ad absurdum* of the proposition that a finite mind can know it possesses adequate knowledge of anything.

The argument Descartes presents to Burman (lines 4–12) can be summarized as follows. S has adequate knowledge of X if he knows all the properties that really belong to X (this definition is given in the Fourth Replies, AT vii. 220, line 8).[1] But now, if S is not omniscient, it is always possible that for any set of properties

---

[1] 'Omnes proprietates quae sunt in re cognita.' Here at CB 14 the term 'attribute' (*attributum*) is used in place of 'property' (line 8); but the two terms are often used synonymously by Descartes: cf. AT vii. 383, where Descartes says that 'property' (*proprietas*) is to be taken 'pro quolibet attributo, sive pro omni eo quod de re potest praedicari'.

$F_1 - F_n$ that he knows X to possess, X in fact has a further property, F_{n+1} of which he is ignorant. So although S may *in fact* often possess adequate knowledge of X (i.e. although $F_1 - F_n$ may in fact exhaust the properties of X), S can never know that his knowledge is adequate. Descartes' illustration with the triangle is admirable and self-explanatory.

Descartes' doctrine of adequate knowledge seems to me clear and all of a piece. Frankfurt, however, has argued that 'Descartes gives apparently conflicting accounts of whether or not a finite mind can have adequate knowledge of anything'; according to Frankfurt, Descartes tells Arnauld in the Fourth Replies that adequate knowledge is comparatively easy to come by; whereas he tells Burman in our passage that it is difficult or impossible (FRANKFURT, p. 142). But this is highly misleading. What Descartes actually says to Arnauld is that a finite mind, 'even though it may really have adequate knowledge of many things, cannot however *know* he has such knowledge' (AT vii. 220, lines 12–14). And this is exactly what Descartes says to Burman: it is not adequate knowledge *per se* that is described as difficult or impossible, but merely the certainty that one's knowledge is adequate. The only point in Frankfurt's favour is that at line 6, discussing the triangle 'which it seems we should very easily be able to achieve adequate knowledge of' (rem . . . quam facillime adaequare posse videremur), Descartes adds 'yet none the less we cannot do so' (sed nihilominus illum adaequare non possumus). But what follows makes it clear that the phrase 'illum adaequare non possumus' was just a loose way of talking. The point is *not* that we cannot in fact know all about the triangle, but that we can never be *sure* we know all about it: 'nos nunquam certi simus nos omnia illa comprehendisse quae de ea re comprehendi poterant' (see lines 11/12). The issue is finally clinched at the end of the passage: Descartes says he has never claimed adequate knowledge of anything; but none the less he is pretty convinced that he does in fact possess the sort of knowledge and foundations 'from which adequate knowledge could be—and *perhaps already has been—* deduced' (my italics). By no stretch of the imagination is this the language of one who believes adequate knowledge is 'difficult or impossible' for a finite mind to attain.

Although Descartes may give a clear and coherent account to Burman of his views on adequate knowledge, he does not explain how they help to deal with Arnauld's original objection. Arnauld's question was: 'how does it follow, from the fact that one is not aware of anything, besides thought, that belongs to one's essence, that nothing else does in fact belong to it?' (AT vii. 199). How, in other words, does Descartes know that he has not left out some

vital property of himself? In order to know this, Arnauld had
argued, Descartes would have to know that his knowledge of
himself was adequate (AT vii. 200). Descartes' reply to this,
backed up by the remark to Burman we have discussed, only
seems to make matters worse. One can never, it appears, know
one's knowledge of anything is adequate. But in that case, it
seems that not only has Descartes failed to show how he knows
he has not overlooked some property; he necessarily could not
have succeeded. (See further KENNY (1), p. 95 and MALCOLM, § 11.)
l. 19. who can say? Some rhetorical question of this sort seems
called for here, but the original cannot satisfactorily be recovered
at this point.

CB 15. l. 6: subject-matter for error (*materia erradi*). The
chief and most common error, says Descartes, is to suppose that
an idea resembles or fits some external thing. Error of this sort,
which essentially involves a mistaken judgement (*judicium*), is
called 'falsity proper' or 'formal falsity' (falsitas proprie dicta seu
falsitas materialis; Third Meditation, AT vii. 37 and 43). But
suppose I do not relate the idea to anything extra-mental? In this
case, Descartes goes on to explain, there can still occur another
sort of falsity—'falsity concerning subject matter' or 'material
falsity' (*falsitas materialis*). This occurs when one of my ideas
'represents a non-thing as a thing' (non rem tamquam rem
repraesentat); the idea is then a 'false idea' (*idea falsa*) (AT vii.
43-4; HR i. 164). The example Descartes gives of this concerns
the idea of cold. My idea of cold may represent cold to me as
'something real and positive' (*reale quid & positivum*); whereas
cold in reality is nothing more than a negation—the absence of
heat (*privatio caloris*).
    There is an involved and rather inconclusive exchange about
this between Arnauld and Descartes (AT vii. 206 and 232-3),
which we need not go into; for the comment to Burman at CB 15
shows that material falsity (error concerning ideas alone) does
not arise only in the case of ideas of negations: it can happen with
regard to a non-negative idea like that of whiteness. The example
chosen in the Third Meditation was thus needlessly complicated.
Nevertheless, even with the new example we are still left very
much in the dark. How is it that the idea of whiteness 'represents
a non-thing as a thing'? What exactly is the error in supposing
colour to be a 'thing or a quality' (line 9)? Or again, what on
earth is wrong with supposing whiteness to be a colour (lines
10-11)?
    The answer is that Descartes regards whiteness as what
Locke was later to term a 'secondary' quality (*Essay on Human*

Understanding Bk. II, Ch. 8), viz. merely a subjective effect of certain movements and shapes in the external world. See the letter to Chanut of 26 February 1649, where Descartes says that all sensible qualities apart from size, shape, and movement are 'merely in our senses like a tickle or a pain and not at all in the objects which we perceive' (AT v. 291–2; K 246). Cf. *Principles* IV, 198 (AT viii. 332–3). I owe these references to Adam, who selects this particular piece from the *Conversation* (CB 15) for one of the rare philosophical comments in his edition:

C'est la grande erreur, au sentiment de Descartes, de toute la physique . . . scolastique de se tromper sur la nature des données sensibles en nous, et d'y voir des qualités réelles dans les choses mêmes. Et il ne crut pouvoir mieux ruiner cette physique qu'en supprimant radicalement toutes qualités réelles et formes substantielles dans les corps, n'y laissant subsister comme seule réalité qu'étendue, figure et mouvement [ADAM, ad loc.].

To explain fully what is said to Burman, however, this comment needs to be supplemented by our analysis of the distinction between formal and material falsity. If I judge that there is an extra-mental entity which my idea of whiteness 'fits' (i.e. I judge that whiteness is instantiated), then I am indeed making a mistake; but the mistake involves a judgement about something extra-mental—it is a piece of 'formal falsity'. 'Material falsity', on the other hand, can occur even when I exercise the utmost caution and refrain from making any extra-mental judgement— 'even when I do not say or suppose there exists any white thing' (CB 15, line 13). According to Descartes, the mere fact of mentally classifying whiteness as a 'quality' makes me guilty of error; apparently, just by thinking that 'white' ('sweet', 'loud') belong in the same bag with 'extended' ('square', 'moving'), I am committing myself to what Descartes regards as a thoroughly unscientific prejudice about the structure of the external world.

There is a further reference to 'material falsity' at CB 26, q.v., but the passage is extremely obscure. The opening quotation is from Descartes' reply to the Second Objections. Mersenne and company had objected that Descartes had failed to prove that we have an innate idea of God. The idea, they argued, may just be acquired from one's cultural environment (passed on by books, friends, etc.); and they cited the fact that the 'Canadians, Hurons and other *sylvestres homines*' do not possess any such idea (AT vii. 124). Descartes' apparent counter to this is that people who fashion idols may not verbally acknowledge they have an idea of God, but the very fact that they fashion idols shows that they have it. This at any rate is what seems to be meant by the cryptic sentence 'nomen negant et rem concedunt' (AT vii. 139).

If the quotation from the *Replies* is obscure, the explanatory comment to Burman completely escapes me. Why is the idol 'equivalent to our idea'? Perhaps because, however imperfectly, it 'represents' God (cf. CB 37, line 4). The next sentence is even more difficult, but the sense seems to be that those who fashion idols must in so doing form a real idea, and this idea is materially false. (MS.: 'qua [?] realem formant ideam dum idolum formant, formant ideam materialiter falsam.') If the idea is materially false, this implies that the idea represents a non-thing as a thing (see above). But God is emphatically not a non-thing. Nor can Descartes mean that the bogus god whom the savages worship is a non-thing: for even an imaginary entity like a chimera qualifies as a thing (*res*), which I can have a true idea of (AT vii. 37, lines 3–5; cf. below on CB 34). In any case, if the idea which the idol-makers have is materially false, is not Descartes in effect conceding the point originally urged by Mersenne and company—that not all people have a genuine innate idea of God?

CB 16. l. 5: at this point. The demonstrative adverb '*hic*' occurs frequently in the *Conversation* (cf. CB 1, line 10; CB 11, line 2; CB 17, line 3). When challenged about some assertion in the *Meditations* which appears to conflict with some earlier or later remark, Descartes invariably insists on focusing on the exact context—the precise stage which has been reached in the inquiry. There is an important insight to be had here about the nature of the *Meditations*. We cannot treat them as if they were meant as a piece of straightforward exegesis of Descartes' philosophy in the manner of, say, the *Principles*; we cannot, for example, lift some assertion out of the *Meditations* and assume it represents Descartes' final and considered view. For at any given point Descartes may be dramatically projecting himself into a certain temporary stage in the development of the inquiry. (Compare also the sentence at line 4 of this passage: 'this is only an objection and a doubt that can be raised'.)

CB 17. ll. 15/16: method and order of discovery . . . of exposition. The 'order of discovery' (*ordo inveniendi*) apparently characterizes the individual voyage of discovery as it is dramatically outlined in the *Meditations*; the order of exposition (*ordo docendi*) is represented by the more impersonal and formal approach of the *Principles*. Now, in the following sentence (line 17), Descartes remarks that in the *Principles* his procedure is 'synthetic' (*synthetice agit*); and this suggests that the distinction between the order of discovery and the order of exposition corresponds to a distinction made in the Second Replies between two 'methods of demonstration'—the *analytic* method, and the *synthetic* method.

The method which works through analysis, we are told, 'shows the way by which the thing was discovered methodically'; it enables the reader, if he is ready and willing to follow it, 'to make the thing his own (*suam reddere*) just as much as if he had discovered it himself'. It is the only method used in the *Meditations* (AT vii. 155–6; HR ii. 48–9). The synthetic method, on the other hand, 'demonstrates the conclusion clearly by a long series of definitions, postulates, axioms, theorems, and problems'. The good will of the reader is not required: the conclusion just follows logically, and if the reader is taken through the proof he will see this whether he likes it or not (ibid.).

The simplest way of seeing what Descartes is getting at here is to look at the paradigm case of the synthetic method which he himself provides at the end of the Second Replies. There the proofs of God's existence are drawn up formally, complete with definitions, axioms, and postulates. The order followed is the order of strict logical priority; or, as Descartes sometimes puts it, the order corresponds to the priorities which obtain 'in reality' (*in re ipsa*: references below). This is our 'order of exposition'. But, as we are told at the end of CB 17, the order of discovery may be quite different from this. What this must mean is that the strict logical priority followed in the formal proof need not at all correspond to the order in which the individual arrives at knowledge of God's existence when he follows the method of discovery described in the *Meditations*.

An example of how this can occur is given by Descartes at CB 19. We are able to recognize our own imperfection before we recognize the perfection of God (i.e. when following the order of discovery in the *Meditations*); however, in terms of strict logical priority the perfection of God comes first: 'for in reality (*in re ipsa*) the infinite perfection of God is prior to our imperfections' (lines 19/20). And at CB 4, in closely similar language, Descartes says that the major premiss 'whatever thinks is' is in reality (*in re ipsa*) prior to the inference 'I think therefore I am'. The distinction between formal logical order and order of actual discovery thus turns out to be crucial for Descartes' treatment of the Cogito. (See further Introduction, pp. xxiv ff.)

One further point: the fact that the order corresponding to the synthetic method is called the *ordo docendi* does not mean it is especially suited to teaching. It does have the advantage of compelling assent (AT vii. 156); but given a willing pupil, it is the method of *analysis* that is the 'best and truest method for teaching' (ibid.). So by using the verb *doceo* when talking to Burman about the synthetic method, what Descartes must mean, I think, is not that the method is good for inspiring pupils, but that it is the method for 'exposition'—setting the arguments out formally on a blackboard, as it were; this is why I have translated *ordo docendi* as 'order of exposition'.

CB 18. ll. 4/5: 'idea' in its strict and narrow sense: cf. an earlier passage in the Third Meditation: 'quaedam ex his [cogitationibus] tanquam rerum imagines sunt, quibus solis proprie convenit ideae nomen; ut cum hominum vel Chimaeram vel Coelum vel Angelum vel Deum cogito' (some of my thoughts are as it were images of things, and these alone are, strictly speaking, called ideas; for example, when I think of a man, or a chimera, or heaven, or an angel, or God: AT vii. 37). Elsewhere, however, Descartes uses 'idea' in a much wider sense than this. Sometimes he says that we have an idea of X when we merely know the meaning of the word (or phrase) X. Thus, in the definition given in the Second Replies, my being able to use words intelligently is stated to be a sufficient condition for my having an 'idea' of what the words mean: 'nihil possim verbis exprimere intellegendo id quod dico quin ex hoc ipso certum sit, in me esse ideam ejus quod verbis illis significatur' (AT vii. 160; HR ii. 52; cf. AT iii. 395). This must be what Descartes has in mind when he talks to Burman here at CB 18, line 7 about a 'rather extended' use of 'idea': in this wider sense I can be said to have an idea of a 'common notion' (i.e. a proposition like 'ex nihilo nihil fit'—see note on CB 1, line 7), or an idea of 'nothing', which does not stand for any object of thought but is 'purely negative' (line 3).

Descartes does not say whether we have idea (loose) of 'and', 'but', 'though', etc. A problem here is that Descartes has no very clear principle of individuation for ideas. When I have an idea of brother, and an idea of male sibling, for example, do I have three ideas, or two, or one? Moreover, in the case of a 'common notion', do I have an idea corresponding to each word in the sentence *and* an idea corresponding to the sentence as a whole? Again, we are never told. Nor does Descartes' remark that both words and propositions can express ideas help us much (AT iii. 395; K 106).

CB 19. l. 1: in the *Discourse*, p. 31. The reference is to the Latin version of 1644 (see Introduction, p. xiv); the relevant sentence is: 'evidentissime intellegebam, dubitationem non esse argumentum tantae perfectionis quam cognitionem' (AT vi. 559; HR i. 102).

l. 6. In that part of the *Discourse*: i.e. Part IV. Descartes makes it quite clear to Burman that the *Meditations* are to be regarded as the definitive statement of his metaphysics. Compare the 'Preface to the Reader' published in the first edition of the *Meditations*, where Descartes says that he 'slightly touched on' (*paucis attigi*) questions concerning God and the human mind in the *Discourse* 'not indeed to deal with them in careful detail, but only in passing and so as to learn from the views of readers how they should be dealt with at some later date' (AT vii. 7). Descartes in fact carefully chose the word *Discours* to emphasize the introductory character of the work, as he explains in a letter to Mersenne a few months before publication: 'I do not put *Treatise on the Method* but *Discourse on the Method* which is the same as *Preface* or *Introductory Note on the Method* to show that it is not my plan to teach it, but merely to talk about it' (AT i. 347; K 30). Incidentally, although I have in my translation used the normal English title 'the *Discourse*', at CB 19, lines 1 and 7, in the original Latin both Descartes and Burman refer to the work simply as *Methodus* ('the *Method*').

ll. 11/12. implicitly . . . explicitly: see above on CB 17.

ll. 22/23. every defect and negation presupposes that which it falls short of and negates. Descartes' proof of God's existence in the Third Meditation depends on the crucial premiss that my concept of a perfect God is (implicitly) prior to my concept of my imperfect self. The alleged priority, as we see from the remarks here, is a function of the alleged fact that imperfection is a defect or negation, while perfection is something positive (cf. also CB 39, lines 9–11).

This argument presupposes that there is some neat way of determining which is the positive and which the negative member of a pair of opposite predicates. But in fact it is extremely difficult to find a satisfactory criterion for classifying predicates as positive or negative. One suggestion is given here at line 22: the test for a 'negation' is apparently that it 'presupposes' its positive counterpart. What is meant by this relation of presupposition? A possible answer is that X presupposes Y if in order to have the concept of X one must have the concept of Y, *but not vice versa*. This would make sense of the remark at lines 26/7: in Metaphysics nothingness presupposes being, says Descartes, because 'our understanding of nothingness derives from that of being' (nihil intelligitur per ens): the claim here is, apparently, that in order to understand nothingness one must have the concept of being, but not vice versa. A similar criterion for distinguishing positive from negative predicates has been advanced in our own day by J. L. Austin, in connection with his notion of the 'trouser-word': 'It is usually thought, and I dare say usually rightly thought, that what one might call the affirmative use of a term is basic—that, to understand 'x' we need to know what it is to be x, or to be an x, and that knowing this apprises us of what it is *not* to be x, not to be an x' (AUSTIN, p. 70).

Unfortunately for Descartes, however, this alleged priority or 'basicness for understanding' evaporates under scrutiny of particular cases. It is true that some cases can be cited which make the claim look intuitively plausible, particularly when some sort of defect or privation is involved. Significantly, Descartes' most frequent examples of negations are 'defects' (e.g. error, AT vii. 54) and 'privations' (e.g. cold, AT vii. 233). If we take the pair 'sighted' and 'blind', it might seem plausible to call 'sighted' the 'positive' or 'affirmative' partner; and this may seem to be confirmed by the application of Descartes' test: the concept 'blind' seems to presuppose the concept 'sighted' (in order to understand what 'blind' means, we have to have some concept of what it is to be sighted, while the converse does not seem to hold). But as soon as we depart from such intuitively helpful cases, difficulties multiply. Take the pair 'perfect' and 'imperfect'. Which is the 'trouser-word' here? To understand what an imperfect apple is, it seems I must have the concept of a perfect apple; but the converse seems equally to hold: I could not know what was meant by a perfect apple unless I had the concept of an imperfect apple. There does not seem to be any priority at all here: in order to understand either of the two terms one must understand what is meant by the other. The two terms rank *pari passu*.

ll. 26/7. In Metaphysics . . . being. MS.: 'In Metaph. nihil intelligitur per ens.' For an unexplained reason the copyist has crossed this line out after writing it (there is a diagonal slash through each word); so the text may possibly be suspect—although it makes perfectly adequate sense in the context. Adam prints 'V.' at the beginning of the sentence ('Voir cela en Métaphysique: le néant ne s'entend que par l'être'). But what he has read as 'V' is, I think, simply a badly formed 'R' (signifying, as usual, a reply of Descartes).

CB 20. l. 3 : by knowledge. For the importance of the point about knowledge in the context of the Third Meditation, see CB 21, lines 10–25.

CB 21. Quotation. The key words from the Third Meditation on which Burman wishes to focus are 'nulla difficiliora mihi factu videntur'. In our MS., the second word is misquoted as 'differentia'! Similar inaccuracies in the quotations which head each piece are found in at least three other places in the *Conversation*: CB 18 ('tantum rei' for 'tamquam rerum'); CB 22 ('subjectum' for 'substantiam'); and CB 62 ('quo minima' for 'quo minora'). We can hardly attribute these errors to Burman himself: mistakes like the one here at CB 21 are too gross to have been made by the man who selected the texts for discussion, and who, as his questioning shows, had made a detailed and careful study of the passages involved. It seems most likely that our 'unknown scribe' (see Introduction, p. xii) is to blame.

ibid. (i.e. many forms of knowledge . . .). This gloss is not in the original Latin version of the *Meditations*; I have supplied it from the French version (AT ix. 38).

11. 1/2. understanding, conception, and imagination. This piece should be read in conjunction with CB 42, in which Descartes explains his theory of imagination and also that of sense-perception (*sentire*). The remarks below cover both passages.

We are nowadays in the habit of thinking of Descartes as a 'dualist'—as maintaining a rigid division between the 'mental' and the 'physical'. There is of course truth in this view. But we should be careful not to take it to imply that Descartes believes in two completely distinct sets of operations, bodily operations (e.g. breathing) and mental operations (e.g. doubting), with no logical links between them. For *imagination* and *perception* provide cases of what might be called 'hybrid concepts'—concepts which, according to Descartes, cannot be explicated without reference to both the physical and the mental.

Perception (*sentire*) involves, according to Descartes at CB 42, a relation between mind and body. It is a matter of the mind's attending to (*animadvertere*) images imprinted on a part of the brain—the 'gland' (line 10). This gland, as Descartes explains frequently elsewhere, is the pineal gland (*conarion*) which he regards as the 'principal seat of the soul' (le principal siège de l'âme; letter to Meyssonier, AT iii. 19; K 69). Exactly what is involved in perception is made a little clearer in the *Passions of the Soul* (Part I, Art. 35): when, for example, we see an animal, the light reflected from it 'paints two images on our eyes' (peint deux images, une en chacun de nos yeux); these two images form others (via the optic nerves) in the 'interior surface of the brain'; these then radiate (*rayonnent*) towards the pineal gland, where they eventually merge into a single image; it is this single image which 'acts immediately on the soul and causes it to see the shape of the animal' (agissant immédiatement contre l'âme, lui fait voir la figure de cet animal; AT xi. 355–6).

Descartes had talked about *imagination* at the beginning of the Sixth Meditation, but his remarks there were, to say the least, cryptic. Imagination, it was suggested, is 'some sort of application of the cognitive faculty to a body intimately present to it' (applicatio quaedam facultatis cognoscitivae ad corpus ipsi intime praesens; AT vii. 72); further, it involves a kind of 'inspection of' (*inspicere*) or 'looking at' (*intueri*) some portion of the body resembling an idea (AT vii. 73). The nature of this strange operation of 'inspecting' is left unexplained (the French version of de Luynes offers the vague gloss 'considérer' for *inspicere*). At CB 42, Descartes explains that *inspicere* is a 'special mode of thinking' (specialis modus cogitandi, line 7); and he refers us to another passage in the Sixth Meditation ('page 81', AT vii. 78), where both imagination and perception were called 'faculties for special modes of thought' (facultates specialibus quibusdam modis cogitandi). The nature of imagination is thus closely related to that of perception; and this, it turns out, is because both involve a special sort of causal transaction between mind and brain (pineal gland). As in the case of perception, imagination involves the painting or imprinting of images on the gland; but the difference is that this happens 'with the windows shut, as it were' (CB 42, line 19): the images are painted on the 'gland' not by external objects, but by the mind itself. The mind then inspects or contemplates (*inspicere*) the images it has painted. The use of our brains as little blackboards which we draw on and then contemplate must be among the most bizarre psycho-physical transactions in Descartes' philosophical psychology.

By contrast with imagination, *understanding* (intellegere, intellectio) is a purely mental operation (AT vii. 73, lines 14–20). Two further points of difference are noted by Descartes. First, when I imagine a triangle, I actually 'see' a three-sided figure in my mind's eye (istas tres lineas tanquam praesentes acie mentis intueor; AT vii. 72); but to understand X seems to be simply to be aware of what is meant by the word 'x', to have the concept of X, without 'seeing' any image (cf. letter to Mersenne of July 1641: whatever we conceive of *sans image* is an idea of pure mind; whatever we conceive of *avec image* is an idea of the imagination: AT iii. 395; K 107; see also AT iv. 304; K 178). A second psychological difference noted in the Sixth Meditation is that imagination requires mental effort (*peculiaris animi contentio*, AT vii. 72–3). In the *Conversation* Descartes illustrates this with mathematical concepts: it is impossible to imagine a chiliagon except in a very vague way; and even a heptagon or octagon cannot be pictured except with considerable effort and practice (CB 42, lines 20–27). Descartes is surely wrong, however, if he means to suggest that mental effort is necessarily—or even generally—a feature of imagination. Normally, one is no sooner asked to picture something ('Picture an old man with a grey beard!') than one has done so. And in general, being imaginative is not being good at something difficult and taxing like mental arithmetic: the images just 'come' without any conscious effort. Nor is it the case that mental effort, when it does occur, is peculiar to imagination;

frequently, to come to understand some new concept (e.g. the concept of a cosine) may involve considerable mental effort, even though there is no picturing involved.

If Descartes' use of the terms *intellectio* and *imaginatio* is reasonably clear, this can hardly be said of the third notion introduced at CB 21, viz. *conceptio*. The cognates 'conceive of' and 'conception' in English suggest something closer to purely intellectual than to 'imaginative' cognition: one may be said, for example, to have a 'conception' of God, or of an infinite number, if one understands what is meant by the words in question, even though one cannot frame any corresponding images. Descartes, however, cannot mean this, as we see from lines 3/4. Nor can conception be identified with the strict image-forming of *imaginatio*, though it does involve some kind of internal representation (line 8). What then *is* this form of cognition which is neither pure understanding nor imagination, but, presumably, something in between the two? It seems to me likely that what Descartes had in mind is something like our notion of 'grasping' an idea or concept. Take the idea of a million pigs. This is a notion which I can clearly understand—I am perfectly aware of what is meant. On the other hand, I cannot imagine or picture such a vast number of pigs except in a very vague and confused way; such are the limitations of the human brain. What I can do, however, is to try to *grasp*, or 'get my mind round' the bafflingly large number, so that my conception of what is involved is rather more vivid than the pure and simple understanding of what is meant. One way of going about this might be to think of ten groups of one hundred pigs; then think of this number put together in a field; then think of a thousand such fields. This seems to be the sort of process which Descartes has in mind at CB 21, apropos of conceiving of the infinite perfections of God: e.g. to grasp what is involved in the concept of infinite knowledge, one has to think of possessing a little more knowledge than one has at present, and then a little more again than this new amount, and so on (cf. lines 10–18). To *conceive of* X, then, is to have what may be called a dynamic working knowledge of what X involves. That Descartes' *conceptio* should be interpreted along these lines is suggested by an interesting passage in a letter to Mersenne of 1630: 'one can *know* (savoir) that God is omnipotent and infinite even though our mind, being finite, cannot *comprehend* (comprendre) or *conceive of* (concevoir) him, just as we can touch a mountain with our hands but not grasp it (embrasser); for . . . *comprehending* is grasping with one's thought (embrasser de la pensée), whilst in order to *know* something, one merely has to touch it with one's thought (toucher de la pensée) (AT i. 152; K 15; italics mine).

ll. 19/20. indefinites . . . infinite: for this distinction, see below on CB 51.

CB 22. Burman has not yet exhausted his quotations from the Third Meditation proper; so the placing of CB 22 before CB 23 and CB 24 is a departure from the normal procedure followed in the section CB 1–48.

l. 6. attributes are the same as the substance. Cf. *Principles* I, 63: 'thought and extension can be regarded as constituting the natures of understanding substance and bodily substance; and then they must not be considered in any other way than as thinking substance itself and extended substance itself, that is, as mind and body' (cogitatio et extensio spectari possunt ut constituentes naturas substantiae intellegentis et corporeae; tuncque non aliter concipi debent quam ipsa substantia cogitans et substantia extensa, hoc est quam mens et corpus). Here we seem to be offered the equations:

$$\text{cogitatio} = \text{substantia cogitans} = \text{mens}$$
$$\text{extensio} = \text{substantia extensa} = \text{corpus}$$

Against this, however, one may set the frequent passages where Descartes follows the traditional doctrine of substance as something underlying attributes—the 'substrate' immortalized by Locke as 'something we know not what'. Elsewhere in the *Principles*, for example, Descartes talks of the 'common notion', 'nihili nulla sunt attributa', in virtue of which we conclude, on perceiving an attribute, that there is necessarily some substance present, to which it may be attributed (I, 52). Again, the definition in the Second Replies (quoted at CB 25) seems clearly to imply that what we are immediately aware of (thought) must be located *in* something, viz. a substance. And the comment which Descartes adds at CB 25 makes his commitment to the traditional doctrine absolutely explicit. As well as the 'attribute which specifies the substance', he tells Burman, one must think of the 'substance itself which is the substrate of that attribute' (praeter attributum quod substantiam specificat debet adhuc concipi ipsa substantia, quae illi attributo substernitur). Compare also CB 43, lines 4–5: since thought is an attribute, says Descartes, you may ask the question, 'What substance does it belong to?' (cui substantiae conveniet?).[1]

---

[1] My talk of the 'traditional' theory of substance (involving the notion of a substrate underlying qualities) runs afoul of a claim by G. E. M. Anscombe that the doctrine of the 'propertyless subject', though not precisely a straw man ('real humans have gone in for it'), is nothing like what philosophers who employ the term 'substance' have generally meant by it (ANSCOMBE, p. 71). In the case of Descartes and the famous piece of wax, Anscombe

How then are we to reconcile these texts with the passage at CB 22, and the apparent identification of *cogitatio* and *mens* at *Principles* I, 63 ? A first step is to focus on a phrase from the remark to Burman at CB 25 quoted above, viz. 'attribute which specifies the substance'. What Descartes seems to be saying is that, although one must acknowledge that the mind is a substance plus accidents, the attribute of thought does in an important sense pick out or define the substance. This is confirmed by another passage from the *Principles*: 'there is always one chief property of any substance which *constitutes its nature* and essence, and on which all the others depend' (I, 53; italics mine). In the light of this, it seems that Descartes' true position is represented by a modified equation:

$$\left.\begin{array}{l}\text{cogitatio}\\\text{extensio}\end{array}\right\}\begin{array}{l}\text{specifies}\\\text{constitutes nature of}\\\text{defines}\end{array}\left\}\begin{array}{l}\text{mens — substantia cogitans}\\\text{corpus — substantia extensa}\end{array}\right.$$

This to a large extent accounts for the original difficult passage from *Principles* I, 63, where we indeed find that thought (extension) is said to *constitute the nature* of thinking (extended) substance. But following immediately after this we have the sentence 'and then they must not be considered in any other way than as thinking substance itself and an extended substance itself', which still remains a problem. For, on the face of it at least, being the attribute which constitutes the nature and essence of X is not precisely the same as being identical with X. The curious way in which Descartes has expressed himself here does seem to make it very hard for us to decide whether mental substance is, or is not, to be regarded as distinct from thought.

The answer to this is, I think, that the imprecision is in a certain sense deliberate. In order to explain this, we have to realize that, for Descartes, the distinction between a substance and its attributes—or, more precisely, a substance and its *defining* or *essential* attributes—was a conceptual rather than a 'real' one. At *Principles* I, 62, the distinction between a substance and its defining

offers an analysis of the argument which 'does not lead to the characterless substrate which people supposed was meant by "substance" '. The conception of substance implied by the wax passage, according to Anscombe, *includes* the essential properties of the wax: 'Descartes' argument . . . does not require a propertyless subject, but a subject with some permanent properties . . .'. Now, as I am in process of arguing, Descartes' notion of substance vacillates considerably, and does indeed come near, at times, to including—in fact almost being identified with—essential properties. Nevertheless, the passages from the *Conversation* quoted above make it clear that Descartes was aware of—and prepared at times to subscribe to—a traditional doctrine of substance as the substrate over and above (or rather under and beneath) essential properties.

attribute is called a *distinctio rationis*: by this phrase Descartes means a theoretical distinction (French version: 'une distinction qui se fait par la pensée'), which is to be contrasted with a real distinction—a *distinctio realis* (for these terms see further on CB 36, below). The matter is made even clearer in our vital passage at CB 22, where Descartes (subject to a minor caveat) baldly accepts Burman's suggestion that the attributes of something and the substance are *identical* (attributa sunt idem cum substantia; line 4). Descartes' view, as the subsequent remarks show, is that when you have created all the attributes of a thing you have *eo ipso* created the substance. The only caveat is that 'creating all the attributes' must be understood to mean 'creating them *all together*', as opposed to separately and individually (lines 7/8). The substance, in real terms, is identical with the attributes provided they are 'taken together' (*collective sumpta*, line 7).

This goes a long way towards explaining Descartes' irritation with Gassendi in the Fifth Replies. Gassendi had objected to Descartes' claim to have discovered the true nature of the wax, in the Second Meditation. We may know that something underlies the changing shapes etc., Gassendi had argued, but we have no real conception of the 'nuda et occulta substantia' (AT vii. 273). In his reply (AT vii. 359) and the explanatory comment offered to Burman at CB 13, Descartes reacts strongly to the suggestion that he 'abstracted' the concept of the wax from that of its attributes. The investigation revealed that the wax was never without accidents: particular accidents may have disappeared but others always took their places. This comment, coupled with the remarks at CB 22, strongly suggests that Descartes did not subscribe to the real existence, behind observable properties, of a 'naked and hidden substance'. Though the wax may take on various shapes and forms, these are all modifications of the defining attribute of extension; and since there is 'in reality' no distinction between the substance and its defining attribute, in discovering the various 'modes of extension' of the wax, we have, according to Descartes, discovered all there is to discover about the wax. There is not extension *plus* some hidden substance; we may of course make a theoretical distinction and say that the extension 'constitutes the nature of the substance'; but in reality the two are identical: the extension is 'the very substance'. And the same, *mutatis mutandis*, is true of the mind.

l. 8. So it is a greater thing. My translation is a rather free version of the original, which is somewhat chaotic here: 'sic majus est producere substantiam qu[am] attributa s[cilicet] ulla ex attributis, vel nunc unum nunc aliud, et sic omnia & singula'. Descartes' comments to Burman show that the original passage in the

Second Replies should be translated 'it is a greater thing to create *a* substance . . .' rather than 'to create substance . . .' (as HR ii. 57).

CB 23. l. 10: prior to its effects. This is the first of two objections which Burman offers to the idea of creation from eternity (for the second, see below on line 19). Descartes, in his reply, apparently rejects the thesis that a cause must be prior to its effects. He cites, as a counter-example, the decrees (*consilia*) of God. The point, presumably, is that these are caused by God (they are just as much acts as the creation, lines 14–16), yet God is not prior to them: they are eternal, like God himself.

Yet the counter-example seems a very odd one. For God's decrees are surely not *effects of* (causal productions of) God, but rather *part of* him. Indeed, Descartes himself says at CB 21 that they are identical with God (*ejus decreta sunt idem cum ipso*, line 6; cf. CB 50, lines 16 ff.); and if *X* is not logically distinct from *Y*, then surely *Y* cannot be the cause (in any normal sense) of *X*. In fact Descartes admits, in the Fourth Replies, that it is a necessary condition of some things counting as an efficient cause that it be distinct from its effect; but he goes on to say that the *positiva essentia* of something may be regarded as its cause in an extended sense which is analogous to that of an efficient cause (*quae per analogiam ad efficientem referri possit*). It is in this extended sense (more or less equivalent to an Aristotelian 'formal cause') that God is the cause of himself (*causa sui*), and also presumably of the decrees which are 'identical with him' (AT vii. 240 ff.; HR ii. 108 ff.).

But to show that there are causes in an extended or analogous sense (=formal causes) that need not be prior to their effects is hardly to refute Burman's original objection. For God, *qua* creator of the universe, is surely its efficient cause in the strict sense (Descartes himself often uses the phrase when talking of God's relation to the universe, e.g. AT v. 54); and an efficient cause *proper* must surely precede its effects. In fact, however (though this point is not made explicit in the *Conversation*), Descartes rejects temporal priority as a requirement even for efficient causation proper: 'The light of nature does not require with regard to an efficient cause that it be prior to its effect; on the contrary, a thing is not strictly entitled to be called an efficient cause except during the time that it is producing its effect, and hence is not prior to it' (First Replies: AT vii. 108; HR ii. 14).

ll. 17/18. something new happening to God. Since God, by definition, cannot undergo change, the decision to create the universe must be part of him from eternity. This does not necessarily imply that the decision is actualized from eternity; Descartes is not maintaining the thesis that the created universe is *in fact* infinitely old—he denies as much at CB 6. The argument merely shows that there is no logical impossibility in the supposition. Descartes here follows the orthodox Thomist view (*Cont. Gent.* II, 38). Cf. letter to Chanut of June 1647: AT v. 52–3; K 221–2.

l. 19. infinite number. Burman's second objection to creation from eternity is that this would entail an 'infinite number' (sc., of elapsed moments prior to the present). The argument he has in mind appears to be something like that later developed by Kant in the First Antinomy (thesis): 'If we assume that the world has no beginning in time, then up to every given moment an eternity has elapsed, and there has passed away in the world an infinite series of successive states of things. Now the infinity of a series consists in the fact that it can never be completed through successive synthesis . . .' (A 426; B 454; trans. SMITH). An eternal universe, then, would involve the completion of an infinite series, which is absurd. Against this Descartes simply observes (lines 20 ff.) that there is nothing wrong with an infinite series here; we should understand past eternity (*eternitas a parte ante*) just as we do future eternity (*eternitas a parte post*), viz. as an infinite series stretching back into the past, just as future eternity is regarded as an infinite series stretching forward into the future. In neither case is the series complete.

At line 26, Burman comes back: surely past eternity, unlike the future, is actualized—the divisions are 'actual and all at once'. The point seems to be that an infinite series is objectionable in the case of the past, because the fact that the past is actualized (has already actually occurred) means that, if the universe is eternal, an infinite series of events *has already occurred*; and this does seem to 'complete the infinite'. Compare the following defence of Kant's argument by A. C. Ewing: 'The events prior to, say, midday yesterday by Greenwich time are undoubtedly completed by now. They are all over, they are past. But if the world has no beginning, those events are infinite in number. Therefore an infinite number of events have been completed, and we still have a case of the completed infinite' (EWING, p. 212).

In his reply to Burman, Descartes points out that the divisions of past eternity are not 'actualized all at once' (*actu simul*, line 29). By this rather cryptic remark he means, I think, that even though all moments in the past have already actually occurred, it does not follow that we have to regard them *all together* as constituting a completed *set*; that is, although every event in the series is completed, the series itself is not completed or closed. Ewing's defence of Kant is in fact open to a similar reply. Granted that an infinite number of events has elapsed prior to midday yesterday, and all past events are 'completed' ('all over'), it does not at all follow that the *set* of past events has been completed.

ll. 34/5. parts . . . would be separated: so that, even if I exist from eternity, a God is still logically required as the conserver of my existence. See Third Meditation (AT vii. 48; HR i. 168) and Axiom II in the Second Replies: 'no less a cause is required to conserve a thing than was required to produce it in the first place' (AT vii. 165).

l. 39. offence to the Schoolmen (*pedagogi*) '*les pédants*'— Adam. For Descartes' extreme caution in avoiding disputes on theological issues see below on CB 78. There is a further reference to the 'Schoolmen' at CB 80, q.v.

CB 24. l. 2. in his image? The proposition from the Third Meditation which Burman quotes here had been criticized by Gassendi in the Fifth Set of Objections. In general, Gassendi had argued, a product no more resembles its maker than the walls of a house resemble their builder. The only exception is the case of 'generatio per communicationem naturae' (i.e. ordinary parenthood); but this is not how God created us: we are not his offspring; he made us *secundum ideam*, like the builder (AT vii. 306; HR ii. 173). In his reply (also cited here by Burman) Descartes had remarked that divine creation is closer to natural than to artificial creation (i.e. God's relation to us is, *pace* Gassendi, more like that of a begetter than a builder); exactly in what sense this is so is, however, left unexplained. Descartes had also added, rather feebly, that a product does *sometimes* resemble its maker, as in the case of a self-portrait by a sculptor. All this proves, of course, is that such resemblance is possible, not that it is necessarily or even probably involved in the relation between maker and product.

In re-defending his position here in the *Conversation* Descartes does not fare much better than he had done earlier, in the *Replies*. The common axiom 'effectus similis est causae' (cited at line 3) just seems straightforwardly false: the fist that causes a black eye is not itself black; and Burman is quick to resurrect the old counter-example of the house and the builder. In reply, Descartes explains that in this context he is taking *cause* in a very special sense: he is talking of the 'total cause' ('*causa totalis*', line 12).

This phrase occurs in the more precise statement of the 'axiom of causation' to be found in the Third Meditation: 'iam vero lumine naturali manifestum est tantumdem ad minimum esse debere in causa *efficiente et totali* quantum in ejusdem causae effectu' (AT vii. 40, my italics; HR i. 162. Cf. AT vii. 366; HR ii. 217). In a letter to Mersenne (AT iii. 284; K 91) Descartes explains that he added the word *totalis* to exclude obvious counter-examples: the rain and sun are not the *total causes* of the living things they are said to generate, and that is why there is no resemblance. There is a philosophically important point here. When we say that *A* causes *B* (depressing a switch causes the light to go on), we normally mean not that *A* on its own is causally sufficient for the occurrence of *B*, but only that it is sufficient given a set of assumed 'background conditions' (power supply, wiring, light-bulb, etc.). To give the *total cause* of *X*, in Descartes' sense, is thus to specify fully the set of conditions which taken together are causally sufficient for *X*.

Unfortunately, the axiom in its most precise form still seems straightforwardly false. A mixture of sodium and chloride, when compounded in a certain way, is the total cause of salt; yet the salt does not resemble the constituent elements. Descartes' main argument in support of the axiom is that 'nothing comes from nothing': how can we explain the fact that an effect *X* has some property *F* unless *X* gets its *F*ness from its cause? And how could the cause bestow the property *F* unless it possessed it itself? (cf. AT vii. 40: 'quomodo illam [realitatem] ei causa dare posset nisi etiam haberet'). It is the last step in this strangely aprioristic piece of reasoning that is the faulty one. The assumption (which the example of the chemical reaction disproves) is that the only way in which some property may be generated or acquired is by being passed on from a previous owner, like an heirloom. If the reply to this is that the new property must have been present 'potentially', or in some other way, in its causal antecedents, then this preserves the resemblance thesis at the cost of making it trivial and unfalsifiable: an effect will be allowed to be 'like' its cause, even though there is no feature in common. It may be that Descartes has some such (unsatisfactory) reply in mind when he says that the cause of a stone may contain the features of a stone 'vel formaliter vel eminenter' (either literally or in some higher form; AT vii. 41; cf. AG p. 81 and AT vii. 104).

l. 17. be being and substance (*esse ens et substantia*). Resemblance, one would have thought, must be a matter of two substances having an attribute or attributes in common; the mere fact that they are both *substances* will hardly introduce any similarity. Descartes cannot reply here that there are general features which all substances have in common *qua* substances, for he himself asserts at *Principles* I, 51, that the word 'substance' does not apply univocally to God and his creatures. (For the term 'ens', see below on CB 34.)

CB 25 and 26. For these two pieces, see above on CB 22 and CB 15 respectively.

CB 27. l. 1: could not have any force for an atheist. It is not at all clear why Descartes says that the argument could not 'valere apud atheum'; especially since, in the original passage in the Second Replies, the conclusion was said to follow necessarily simply from the premiss that one cannot arrive at a greatest number (AT vii. 139). Now this premiss is clearly one everyone must accept (it does not depend on theistic or any other special assumptions); and if Descartes believes that the conclusion follows as a matter of logical necessity, then surely the argument must have force for *anyone*, atheist or no. (Compare Descartes' own view that valid reasoning 'compels assent'; AT vii. 69 and 145.) It is true that the argument at best proves that there is a being more perfect than myself; not that this being is God (see line 16). So it is not enough to *convert* the atheist, if that is what Descartes means by 'valere'.

CB 28. I have punctuated this piece differently from Adam (see Introduction, p. xv). Adam gives the whole first section to Burman; but it seems better to give the authoritative opening remarks to Descartes, with Burman breaking in to raise a difficulty at line 6. (MS.: 'Sed sic angelus et mens nostra erunt idem.' For 'sed sic' introducing an objection, cf. CB 24, line 19, where the MS. reads: 'sed sic et lapis etc. habebunt imaginem Dei'.)
l. 1. idea of an angel. Descartes had explained in the Third Meditation (AT vii. 43) that my ability to form ideas of angels, other men, and animals does not require me to posit the extra-mental existence of such things as causes of the ideas, since I can construct them out of my ideas of myself and of God. For Descartes, an angel is simply a disembodied mind; hence my idea of myself *qua* 'res cogitans' provides all I need in order to form the idea of one.
ll. 6/7. identical with our mind. Burman here acutely raises what is really a general difficulty for Cartesian dualism, viz. the problem of how mental substances are to be numerically differentiated. The principle we use for individuating physical objects is straightforward enough (spatio-temporal continuity provides the ultimate criterion), but what is it that makes two minds distinct? This problem is examined by D. M. Armstrong in his book *A Materialist Theory of the Mind*, and, interestingly enough, he illustrates the point at issue by referring to Aquinas' treatment of angels:

Angels are disembodied intelligences, and therefore raise the question what makes them numerically different from each other. Aquinas' solution was to say that each angel was of a separate species, a different *sort* of object from any other angel. (See *Summa Theologica*, Pt. I, Q. 50, Art. 4.) Among angels, difference of number is simply a difference of kind. But Aquinas' resolution of the difficulty is clearly a makeshift. Why should not God create two identical angels? It is surely an intelligible possibility. And what would differentiate the two then? [ARMSTRONG, p. 28]

In his comments to Burman, Descartes seems to want to follow Aquinas' solution (lines 11/12). But when he goes on to dismiss the problem, remarking scathingly that nothing Aquinas tackled was more pointless than his treatment of angels, he shows that he has failed to grasp the logical importance of what is at stake. The problem is not just an abstruse theological puzzle; it demands attention, if Descartes is to be able to provide an adequate principle of individuation that will differentiate *any* two mental substances, human as well as angelic.

In fact Descartes never, so far as I know, gave any systematic attention to the problem of providing a logical criterion of personal identity within his system. In so far as he does consider the problem, it is from the subjective or epistemological viewpoint. Each of us knows he is an individual because he has an idea of himself from which he can 'exclude' the idea of any other substance, mental as well as physical: 'from the mere fact that each of us understands he is a thinking thing, and can in his thought exclude from himself every other substance, whether thinking or extended, it is certain that each of us, when regarded in this way, is in reality distinct from every other thinking substance and every bodily substance' (*Principles* I, 60). But a serious difficulty is concealed here. It may be that I can exclude from myself the idea of another extended substance, since I can (supposedly) know a body does not belong to my essence (see above on CB 14). But how can I exclude the idea of another thinking substance? Not, clearly, by excluding thinking from my essence; only, it would seem, by excluding *your* (or anyone else's) thinking from my essence. But how can I do this unless I have some independent way of individuating mental substances?

CB 29. l. 1: never argue from ends (*argumentari a fine*). One of Descartes' reasons for this rule is that it is rash and insulting to God to attempt to delve into his purposes (lines 6/7). Descartes explains to Gassendi (in the passage from the Fifth Replies which Burman here refers to) that in ethics, where conjecture is allowed, we may perhaps be able to speculate about God's plan for the universe; but in the exact physical sciences it is futile to try and discover how each particular phenomenon fits into the divine plan (AT vii. 375).

But, as the criticisms of Aristotle show (lines 4/5), Descartes' strictures are not confined to explanations based on *divine* purposes. There is another, more general objection to teleological explanation which Descartes puts to Burman: even if we can discover the purpose or end of *X*, we are no nearer to knowing the nature of *X* itself (cognito finis non inducit nos in cognitionem ipsius rei, line 3). This comment is extremely revealing. For Descartes, to understand *X* fully is necessarily to have a full mechanical account of its workings in terms of efficient causality. (At *Principles* I, 28, Descartes makes it explicit that his programme is the replacement of final by *efficient* causes.) Knowledge of the purpose and function of, say, the liver just does not qualify as *cognitio ipsius rei*—knowledge of the thing itself: only a mechanical explanation of the workings will do. (See further, on CB 73.)

l. 9. as a philosopher. I have throughout translated *philosophus* and *philosophia* by their English cognates, although there are many places in the *Conversation*, and elsewhere in Descartes, where our terms 'scientist' and 'science' are really closer to what is intended (cf. CB 73, CB 82). Of course, until comparatively recently, 'Philosophy' was universally understood to include the natural sciences, as well as subjects like metaphysics and ethics.

CB 30. The argument depends on the maxim 'nothing in the effect which was not previously in the cause' (see above on CB 24; cf. also Third Meditation: 'if we suppose something to be found in an idea that was not in its cause, it will have it from nothing': AT vii. 41).

CB 31. l. 1: considered in this abstract way. Burman questions the thesis put forward in the Fourth Meditation that the will of man is quite perfect. God's will may be stronger and more efficacious, Descartes had argued, but my will *qua* will ('in se formaliter et praecise spectata') is perfect (AT vii. 57, line 20). Burman, quite reasonably, picks up this rather obscure notion of 'will regarded formally and precisely in itself'. At lines 11–14 he points out that our will may vary in force: sometimes we have a volition proper; sometimes a mere inclination, or 'velleity'. It is not entirely satisfactory for Descartes to explain this variation in degree by reference to ignorance (lines 22 ff.); for presumably, as goods vary in their importance, so (even for a man with complete knowledge) will one's inclination to pursue them. Descartes, however, when he talks of perfection of the will, is not referring to the degree of strength of our inclination, but simply to the power to do or abstain (i.e. affirm or deny, pursue or shun) in any given case (AT vii. 57; HR i. 175). This alleged ability or power to act independently clearly does not admit of degree; it is something we either do or do not possess.

l. 20. operation of the will. Burman's objection shows expert knowledge of the Fourth Meditation. The judgements I make when I err are called acts of the will (*actus voluntatis*, AT vii. 60); the errors which I make are not due to a fault in the intellect, which simply 'perceives ideas which are subjects for judgement' (per solum intellectum percipio tantum ideas de quibus iudicium ferre possim, nec ullus error proprie dictus in eo . . . reperitur; AT vii. 56). Descartes thus seems to have got himself into a terrible muddle: his desire to defend the complete perfection of the will leads him to say that any alleged imperfection depends on faulty judgement; but now, on his own account in the Fourth Meditation, judgement itself turns out to be an operation of the will. The resolution offered to Burman at lines 23–5 which makes intellectual ignorance ultimately responsible for error seems to contradict the passage just quoted from the Fourth Meditation where the intellect, *qua* simple perceiver of ideas, was said to be free from error.

Descartes can be rescued, however, as follows: the intellect, though it is free from error in that whatever it clearly and distinctly perceives is true, none the less is imperfect in that there are many things which it does *not* clearly and distinctly perceive; error arises when the judgement, which should withhold assent in such unclear cases, jumps in and gives assent. This is what Descartes means when he says that error is due to the fact that the will 'extends further than the intellect' (latius patet voluntas quam intellectus; AT vii. 58). For some general problems in Descartes' theory of judgement see KENNY (2), p. 2 ff. For more on the relation between will and intellect, see below on CB 32, line 21.

ll. 26/7. go down deep into himself (*descendat unusquisque in semetipsum*). The ultimate Cartesian appeal to 'inner awareness' as proof of freedom (cf. CB 32, line 11, and Introduction, p. xxxvi). **CB 32.** The main burden of the Fourth Meditation is to reconcile the fact that human beings are liable to error with the benevolence of God and the possibility of attaining true knowledge. Descartes' solution to the problem (summed up in the passage quoted here by Burman) is that we are always free to withhold assent from any proposition whose truth we do not clearly and distinctly perceive; and that such careful withholding of assent ensures avoidance of error.

Burman's objection to this crucial proposition seems to be that it is inconsistent with the theological doctrine of original sin; the subsequent discussion shows that this must be what is behind his rather cryptic question at lines 1–5. Burman is saying in effect: 'If the will is free and "autonomous" (*sui juris*) in the way you suggest, we ought *always* to be able to avoid error by your method —even in moral and supernatural matters: yet this, the Church teaches, is impossible.'

With regard to the moral sphere, the objection seems to be that if we are in doubt whether to obey some rule or precept, the Cartesian rule 'withhold assent' will not help us to avoid error; for indifference in the moral (as opposed to the theoretical) sphere is itself a fault (lines 13 ff.). (A saintly man, for example, pursues the good without any indifference: letter to Mesland, AT iv. 117; K 150. For 'indifference' see Introduction, p. xxxvii.) The same holds good in the case of 'supernatural matters' (line 3; presumably, these are the theological truths we need to acknowledge in order to be saved). Again, withholding assent cannot ensure immunity from error, since the withholding of assent to the relevant truths is itself a sin.

Descartes is characteristically chary of dealing with the theological issue: he acknowledges his commitment to the doctrine of original sin and redemption through grace (lines 17–20), but he does not really make any attempt to discuss the alleged clash between these doctrines and his own thesis in the Fourth Meditation about avoidance of error through suspension of judgement. But in fact it seems to me that his thesis can survive perfectly intact, since the supposed difficulty depends on an illegitimate shift between two senses of the verb *errare*—'to err' or 'go astray' —which is used throughout the Fourth Meditation. By withholding assent from some moral precept or article of faith we may indeed 'go astray' in the moral sense of 'do wrong'; but the Cartesian thesis under discussion was about going astray in the *factual* sense of assenting to a false proposition. The thesis that we can always avoid this sort of 'propositional error' by withholding assent whenever the truth is not clearly and distinctly perceived, is thus quite compatible with the theological doctrine of the need for grace to avoid *moral* error or sin.

ll. 7/8. as he is now in his natural condition. My translation follows the MS., which reads: 'sufficit Philosophus hominem consideret prout in naturalibus suis iam est'. Adam suggests an emendation: 'prout in naturalibus sui juris est', and translates 'dans son état naturel, en tant qu'il ne relève que de lui'. This makes Descartes pick up Burman's phrase *sui juris* (autonomous) at line 4. But the original text, though somewhat cryptic, makes perfectly good sense. Moreover, the exact phrase *prout iam est* (as he is now) recurs in a closely similar passage at CB 82: 'philosophus naturam ut et hominem solum considerat prout iam est' (the philosopher studies nature, as he does man, simply as it is now; lines 10–11). For the contrast between 'philosopher' and theologian see below on CB 78.

ll. 21/2. no one can pursue evil *qua* evil. An echo of the Socratic thesis 'οὐδεὶς βούλεται τὰ κακά' (*Meno.*, 78 b1). Compare the *Discourse*, Part III, where Descartes says that the will does not tend to pursue or shun anything except in proportion as our intellect represents that thing to the will as good or bad (AT vi. 28; HR ii. 98). One might have expected that this doctrine would have led Descartes, as it did Plato, to deny the phenomenon of 'akrasia' or 'weakness of will': that is, to assert that the intellect is sovereign, and that any wrongdoing must be due to ignorance and therefore in some sense unintentional. (Cf. *Protagoras* 345 e1.) There are in fact definite signs of Descartes' moving in this direction. In the passage from the *Discourse* already referred to, he remarks that 'to act well it is sufficient to judge well' (il suffit de bien juger pour bien faire); defending this claim later to Mersenne, he quotes with apparent approval the maxim 'whoever sins does so in ignorance' (omnis peccans est ignorans); moreover, those to whom Ovid's 'video meliora proboque, deteriora sequor' applies, he calls 'weak minded' (faibles esprits), implying that their fault is intellectual rather than moral (AT i. 366; K 32). Here at CB 32, however, although Descartes repeats the claim that 'sins have their source in ignorance' (peccata fluunt ex ignorantia), he adds the qualifying particle *fere*—'generally' or 'almost always' (line 21). And at line 26, at the end of the piece, he baldly comes out with the proposition that the will can be said to be corrupted by the feelings or emotions (*per affectus*; for Descartes' use of this term cf. AT vii. 74, line 27), which seems to be precisely an assertion of the possibility of weakness of will. The truth of the matter, it seems to me, is that Descartes' philosophical psychology does allow for weakness of will, in the sense of a wilful disregarding of the manifest perceptions of the intellect: one may perversely refuse to assent even to a clear and distinct perception of the intellect. However, the only way in which one may do this, it emerges, is by refusing to attend to or concentrate on the relevant proposition (see letter to Mesland of 2 May 1644, AT iv. 116–17; K 150. Cf. KENNY (2), pp. 22 ff.).

CB 33. This discussion is an important illustration of what may be called Descartes' 'metaphysical voluntarism'—the doctrine that (*a*) all moral propositions and (*b*) all truths of logic and mathematics depend in some special sense on the *will* of God.

(*a*) Descartes is quite explicit about his position on this: God did not create a temporal world because he saw it would be better than an eternal world; rather a temporal world is better than an eternal world *because* God preferred it (AT vii. 432; cf. AT vii. 436). One objection to making X's goodness dependent on X's being willed by God is suggested by G. E. Moore's famous 'open question' argument (MOORE, Ch. I, §§ 10 ff.). Given that we know that X is willed by God, is it not still possible sensibly to ask 'But is it good?' Burman's objection (lines 8–10) is really a variation on this theme: could God really make something absurd or repugnant (e.g. hating him) good, just by commanding it? Descartes replies that God could not now issue such a command (presumably because God is 'immutable'; see CB 50), but who is to say that he could not *have* done so? But this seems to ignore the sting in Burman's objection. The interesting question is not whether God can now issue the command to hate him, but whether, if he *were to* issue it, that would *eo ipso* make hating him right.

(*b*) With regard to the dependence of logical truths on God's will Descartes makes it clear to Burman (lines 3–7) that God is the cause not only of the actual but also of the possible, and of the *simple natures* (e.g. basic unanalysable qualities like extension, shape, motion, etc.; *Regulae* XII: AT x. 418). Moreover, just as X is good because God wills it, and not vice versa, so 'God did not make the angles of a triangle equal to two right angles because it was necessary; rather it is necessary because he made it so' (AT vii. 432; cf. letter to Mersenne 27 May 1630, AT i. 152; K 15). The obvious objection to this conception of logical truths is that it does not explain the 'eternal' and 'necessary' character of such propositions. On the question of eternity, Descartes is perfectly able to reply that the decrees are present with God from all eternity (see above on CB 23). As to 'necessity', Descartes observed to Arnauld that we must not suppose just because *we* cannot conceive of a mountain without a valley, or of one and two not making three, that God could not have brought these things about (AT v. 224; K 236).

CB 34. l. 6: true and immutable essence: reading *immutabilem* for the MS. *intellectivam*, as Adam suggests. The phrase 'vera et immutabilis essentia' is one of Descartes' standard expressions. The explanation Descartes offers here of what it is to be a 'true entity' (*verum ens*) greatly contributes towards an understanding of Descartes' theory of essences in general, and his version of the ontological argument in particular. X is a *verum et reale ens* when it has a true and real nature (vera et realis natura, line 13). In the Fifth Meditation (just before the passage quoted by Burman) Descartes had explained that 'I have innumerable ideas of things (*rerum*) which, even if they perhaps exist nowhere outside me, cannot be said to be nothing', since they 'have their own true and immutable natures' (suas habent veras et immutabiles naturas; AT vii. 64). Later on, in place of the word 'nature', we have the fuller phrase 'determinate nature, essence, or form which is immutable and eternal' (determinata quaedam natura sive essentia sive forma, immutabilis et eterna). Here at CB 34, Descartes makes it quite clear that to be a *verum et reale ens* it is not necessary to 'exist' in the sense of being around in the world. The objects of mathematics qualify as *vera entia* even though they only have possible existence, as opposed to the actual specific existence in space which the objects of physics enjoy (lines 13 ff.). Thus, to speak of God, or a triangle, as a *verum et reale ens* is not at all to commit oneself to the actual existence of either of these things (though, in the special case of God, it does of course turn out that existence is deducible from his essence); some of Descartes' critics misunderstood him on this point (e.g. Gassendi; AT vii. 323).

But what are the criteria for being a *verum ens* (or having a true essence)? The remarks which Burman here quotes from the Fifth Meditation suggest that the relevant test is the possession of (logically) demonstrable qualities. This runs into two problems. First there is the trivial counter-example of the round square, of which properties (indeed every property whatsoever) can be demonstrated. To rule this out we have to stipulate—as Descartes implicitly does here at CB 34—that a *verum ens* must not be self-contradictory; i.e. it must be logically capable of existing (see lines 18/19). A second and more disturbing objection is that properties can be logically demonstrated of an existing lion (e.g. that it exists); yet an existing lion is given, along with a winged horse and a triangle inscribed in a square, as an example of something whose nature is 'fictitia et ab intellectu composita' (First Replies, AT vii. 117; HR ii. 20).

This phrase suggests that we are not allowed to 'lump together' any two ideas, and assume that there will be a corresponding *ens verum*, with a true essence. Here in the *Conversation*, however, we are told that anything that can be clearly and distinctly conceived in a chimera is an *ens verum* (lines 4/5); yet one would have thought that a chimera provided a paradigm case of a 'composite and fictitious' entity. Worse still, in the passage from the First Replies where a triangle inscribed in a square was put forward as having a composite and fictitious nature, we are later told that the *combination* of the triangle and the square has just as true and immutable a nature as the triangle alone or the square alone (non minus vera et immutabilis erit ejus [conjunctionis] natura quam solius quadrati vel trianguli; AT vii. 118).

What are we to make of this apparently hopeless contradiction?

I do not think Descartes can ultimately be acquitted of confusion on this issue; but the remarks here in the *Conversation* do at least do something to pinpoint the problem. The crucial point about a *verum ens*, it appears, is that its component parts must be in some way *linked*. Even though we may vividly imagine the head of a lion joined to the body of a goat, we do not clearly perceive the link between the two (line 24). By a 'link' (*nexus*) it seems Descartes must mean an analytic link: 'Peter standing' does not qualify as a *verum ens* because 'I do not clearly see that standing is contained in and conjoined with Peter' (non video clare stare contineri et connexum esse cum Petro; lines 26/7). The requirement of 'containedness' (so reminiscent of the Kantian test for analyticity), must surely be there to rule out purely contingent links.

The notion of an analytic link fits well with the remark in the First Replies that when two ideas cannot be separated by a 'clear and distinct operation of the intellect' we can be sure that we have a true nature and not a composite (loc. cit.). But it is just here that Descartes' confusion seems to arise. For of course it is quite possible that there may be an analytic link between a composite idea *AB* and some feature *F*, even though the elements of the composite, *A* and *B*, are not themselves analytically linked. This seems to explain Descartes' strange contortions over the triangle inscribed in a square. For there are properties which are analytically true of the composite figure (e.g. that the area of the square is twice that of the triangle—Descartes' own example), even though there is no analytic connection between the triangle *per se* and the square *per se*. Similarly, though the components of a chimera are not themselves analytically linked, there are certain properties which are analytically true of the whole composite—e.g. the possession of a lion's head.

Descartes seems to face an impossible dilemma here. On the one hand, a composite like a triangle inscribed in a square seems to be a genuine object of mathematics, with demonstrable properties, so it seems that it cannot be excluded from the class of *vera entia* (cf. CB 34, lines 9–12). On the other hand, to allow composites whose elements are not themselves analytically linked as *vera entia* paves the way for the introduction of composites like Petrus standing, or the existing lion; but this will sabotage the structure of the ontological argument, by eliminating the supposed special status of the idea of God, and making it possible to 'prove' the existence of any arbitrary composite which we choose to invent (e.g. the existing unicorn).

ll. 8/9. when it is merely our supposition that it exists (*cum nos illud existere supponimus*). A difficult clause: Adam translates 'lorsque son existence n'est qu'une supposition de notre esprit'. The stress is on the emphatic *nos* rather than on *existere*; moreover, *existere* in this context is used to mean not 'exist extra-mentally' but 'exist as an *ens*' (have an essence). Descartes does *not* mean that a triangle becomes an *ens fictum* if we suppose it to exist extra-mentally; or that a 'fictitious entity' like a winged horse is only fictitious when we suppose it exists extra-mentally. The point is rather (see the discussion above) that in the case of an *ens fictum* (e.g. a winged horse) its nature is artificial—it depends on *our* lumping together certain ideas; while in the case of an *ens verum* (triangle, God) there is a true essence independent of our minds. The use of *existere* in this sense (to be an *ens*, to have an essence) may seem strange; indeed, according to Kenny, Descartes always reserves *existere* for actual, extra-mental existence, while *dari* is the term for mere 'being' in the sense of being a subject for predication (KENNY (1), p. 151). It seems to me, however, that the word 'exist' was for Descartes, as indeed it is for us, ambiguous between these two senses. When Descartes wants to make it clear that he is talking of actual, extra-mental existence he often uses the phrase *extra me existere* (AT viii. 64, line 8) or *actu existere* (here, line 16).

Note that *existere* is used again in the sense of existing as an *ens* later in this same piece (line 23): what Descartes must mean is *not* that 'it does not follow from our imagining a goat with a lion's head that one *actually* exists'—for no one could have supposed that *this* followed—but that 'it does not follow from our imagining a lion–goat that such a thing exists as a *verum ens*, or has a true essence'.

l. 14. The only difference. For the difference between mathematics and physics, see below on CB 52, lines 6/7.

l. 30. our own inner awareness (*ex propria conscientia*). Descartes' comment here may seem to support the common criticism of the Cartesian method that clarity and distinctness cannot be satisfactory criteria of truth, since the standards they invoke are purely subjective or psychological. For a discussion of this issue, see GEWIRTH. Clarity and distinctness are defined at *Principles* I, 45.

l. 31. explanations. I follow Adam's suggestion (*dilucidationes*) for filling the lacuna in the MS. For the relevant passages in *Principles* I, see especially paras. 1–10, 43–6, and 66–75.

CB 35. l. 2: they would certainly not be Gods. MS.: 'Imo Dei non essent.' Adam reads 'erunt' to conform with the indicative in line 1; but the word in the MS. is quite clearly 'essent' and the change to the subjunctive makes perfectly good sense. I also read 'essent' at line 13 ('non essent Deus') where the MS. is illegible (Adam here reads the singular 'esset').

ll. 5/6. as a kind of thing . . . as an individual (*specificative . . . individualiter*). The term 'God' implies perfection, and perfection, argues Descartes, implies uniqueness. No, says Burman; for in saying 'God is perfect' we are not using God *individualiter*—to refer to a unique individual (or else the question of uniqueness would be begged); rather we are saying that perfection belongs to the nature of Godhead—to God *qua* kind of thing (*specificative*)—and this leaves open the question of how many individuals are so endowed.

Descartes replies that when we say God is perfect we mean that he has *absolutely every* perfection (omnino omnes perfectiones), and this implies supremacy; and supremacy implies uniqueness, since there cannot be more than one supreme being on pain of contradiction (lines 12 ff.). We may accept the second part of this argument but why should the possession of 'absolutely every perfection' imply supremacy? If Descartes means that, if *X* has all the perfections there are, then necessarily *X* has more perfections than anyone else, his reasoning seems faulty, at any rate as it stands. (It is of course true that *omnipotence* implies supremacy, but if Descartes' argument turns on this particular perfection, why does he not say so explicitly?)

CB 36. In the MS. this piece comes near the end of the pieces dealing with the *Meditations* (just before my No. CB 48). But a prefixed note 'Ad Medit. V' (as well as the context) indicates that it belongs with the pieces relating to the Fifth Meditation, and I have transposed it accordingly.

ll. 4-7. in our thought . . . in reality (*cogitatione nostra . . . reipsa*). Descartes elsewhere distinguishes between a *real* distinction (*distinctio realis*) and a theoretical distinction (*distinctio rationis*—'distinction qui se fait par la pensée'—or *distinctio formalis*). In the former case, two things may be clearly and distinctly perceived apart from one another (e.g. body and mind); in the latter case not (e.g. mind and its defining attribute, thought; cf. above on CB 22). (AT viii. 28–30; ixb. 51–3; vii. 120.)

Here at CB 36, then, Descartes would appear to be saying that the distinction between existence and essence is merely a *distinctio rationis*. But this looks very strange. We can clearly and distinctly perceive the essence of a triangle without supposing that it actually exists; indeed, this is the central feature of Descartes' account of mathematics. Compare the letter to 'Hyperaspistes' where Descartes says that 'the whole essence of a triangle can be correctly understood even if it be supposed that there is in reality no such thing' (AT iii. 433; K 119; cf. CB 34, lines 13 ff.).

What the remark to Burman *may* mean, however, is that in the case of an *actually existing object* there is no real distinction between essence and existence. Some support for this view comes in a letter to an unknown recipient where Descartes says that in the case of a triangle existing *outside our thought*, essence and existence are in no way distinct (AT iv. 350; K 187–8). The question of *priority*, which Burman raises (lines 1–2), is relevant here. Since God, in Descartes' system, is responsible not only for what is actual but also for what is possible (i.e. for essences as well as actual existence; see above on CB 33), he does not create by conferring existence on prior essences: he does not, like Leibniz' God, choose this world from among alternatives which are antecedently possible, prior to his will. Rather, his will creates an 'existing-essence': cf. line 9, 'existence is merely existing essence' (*essentia existens*). See also letter to Mersenne of 27 May 1630: 'il est certain qu'il [Dieu] est aussi bien l'Auteur de l'essence comme de l'existence des créatures' (AT i. 152).

This is all very well, but Descartes still seems guilty of an inconsistency. For even in the case of an *actually existing* thing we can consider it clearly 'sub specie possibilitatis': we can clearly and distinctly perceive all the properties that belong to its 'true and immutable essence', and separate these from the contingent fact of its actual existence. Indeed, this must be so if the ontological argument is to work: for it is only in the case of God that existence belongs to his immutable and true essence.

CB 37. This piece should be read in conjunction with CB 38. According to the passage quoted from the Second Replies, contradictoriness arises only in our thought which joins together inconsistent ideas (in solo nostro conceptu, ideas sibi mutuo adversantes male conjungendi). The French version of the *Objections and Replies* (which Haldane and Ross follow here) completely alters the meaning: 'toute impossibilité . . . consiste seulement en notre . . . pensée qui *ne peut* conjoindre les idées qui se contrarient' (AT ix. 119; my italics). But the original makes much better sense, as the discussion here with Burman shows: the mind *can* join together inconsistent ideas; although, as is made clear in CB 38, one cannot have a clear and distinct idea of the resulting composite. (This last point no doubt explains the over-zealous French emendation: for it is true that the mind cannot *clearly and distinctly* join inconsistent ideas.)

ll. 8/9. things . . . are not inconsistent with each other (*non repugnant sibi res*). Descartes' reason for this assertion, viz. 'omnes existere possunt' (all of them can exist; line 9) is inadequate. The Ptolemaic solar system and the Copernican solar system are both capable of existing, but they are not, to use the Leibnizian term, 'compossible'. To prove that no two things are mutually inconsistent Descartes would need the stronger premiss 'omnes *coexistere* possunt'.

Of course, if X can exist, it does indeed follow that X is not *internally* inconsistent; and it may be that there is a muddle here at CB 37 between the questions 'can any two things be *mutually* inconsistent?' and 'can anything be *internally* inconsistent?' (The Latin phrase 'non repugnant sibi res' is ambiguous in this respect, which could perhaps have confused Burman when he was writing up his notes.) Certainly it is internal consistency which is in point in the original argument in the Second Replies; and at lines 11–12 here, we find Descartes saying that in a contradiction we join together separate things which are not inconsistent *taken on their own* (*seorsim*). Cf. CB 38, lines 5/6.

However, if this is what Descartes means he is still confused, since internal consistency of the conjuncts which generate a contradiction obtains in the case of ideas as well as things. So it seems to me that Burman's original objection (lines 1–3) stands. On no interpretation of Descartes' theory of ideas and 'things' will it be possible for ideas, and impossible for things, to be inconsistent, whether mutually or internally.

CB 38. In the Second Replies, Descartes argues that the fact that I have a clear and distinct idea of God's nature entails that his nature is not self-contradictory; here at CB 38 lines 5–9, Descartes in effect defends a corollary of this thesis, viz. that if X is self-contradictory, I cannot have a clear and distinct idea of X. To assess Descartes' defence, consider the case of a round square. Though we have the concept of a circle and that of a square, we have no corresponding concept of a 'round square'; this is just a phrase we mouth without any clear notion of what is meant. However, if 'ideas' are taken to include propositions as well as concepts (as Descartes sometimes allows—see above on CB 18), there seems no comparable difficulty. If we combine the proposition 'p' and the proposition '$-p$', the resulting compound 'p & $-p$' is not meaningless, it is necessarily false. (Indeed, it is hard to see how one can clearly and distinctly perceive the truth of an analytic proposition without clearly and distinctly perceiving the falsity of its contradictory.)

CB 39. l. 3 : the imperfect triangle. As is clear from the passage quoted from the Fifth Replies, Descartes believes, as does Plato, that the imperfections of the empirical world rule out the possibility that we acquired mathematical ideas via the senses. (Cf. *Phaedo* 74b, 4 ff.: no two lines in the empirical world are perfectly equal. For Descartes' innatism in general see Introduction.) In defending his position against Burman's pertinent criticism, Descartes relies on the (dubious) distinction between positive and negative concepts (lines 9–11); for this see above on CB 19.

l. 6. It provides you with both. In the MS., R is prefixed to this sentence, so that the comment is attributed to Descartes (see Introduction, p. xv). But the correct distribution of dialogue in this piece is made clear by the sense.

CB 40–42. The fact that angels (i.e. disembodied spirits) do not imagine (CB 41) is a logical consequence of the essential role of the body in imagining (CB 40). This role is fully explained in CB 42 (for this passage see above on CB 21, pp. 74–5).

CB 43. l. 1. You cannot ask whether the mind is a substance. Why is the question inappropriate? The remarks to Burman suggest that Descartes thinks there are two possible levels at which one can talk about the mind. Either one can speak of 'mind' (*mens*) as in ordinary speech; or one can use the more technical apparatus of the scholastics, and talk of the *attribute*, 'thought' (*attributum, cogitatio/cogitare*), and the 'spiritual *substance*' (*substantia spiritualis*) to which it 'belongs' (*convenire*) (lines 4–7). For these notions see above on CB 22.

ll. 9/10. distinct from, and incompatible with, corporeal substance. If two substances can be clearly and distinctly perceived apart from one another, they are 'in reality' distinct (cf. above on CB 36). It does not seem to follow from the fact that X and Y are distinct that they are also incompatible (cf. AT iv. 350); but Descartes is here quite explicit that this is so in the case of mind and body (una non solum non involvit alteram sed etiam negat; lines 15/16). The reason for the incompatibility is stated elsewhere: 'We cannot conceive of half a mind, as we can do of even the smallest body, so that their natures can be recognized as not only different but also in some way contrary' (*Synopsis*, AT vii. 13; cf. AT vii. 163).

CB 44. Burman's question puts in a nutshell the most serious difficulty of Cartesian dualism. The problem, as it arises in the passage quoted from the Sixth Meditation is that one does not just *notice* that one's mind is damaged as a pilot sees damage in his ship; rather one *feels* pain. And this suggests that there must be some joining (*conjunctio*), mingling (*permixtio*), or union (*unio*) between mind and body. But how two substances which are not only logically distinct but actually incompatible (CB 43) can be joined in this way is a mystery. The appeal to experience (line 4), of which Descartes is so fond (cf. his treatment of freedom CB 31 line 27; CB 32 line 11), of course proves nothing. The fact that we feel pain etc. when our bodies are hurt is the problem for Descartes, not its solution. Perhaps when he says experience 'cannot be gainsaid' (line 6), Descartes is sadly admitting the existence of a brute fact that just cannot be accommodated within his philosophical system. As far as I know, the remark is his last recorded pronouncement on the mind–body problem. (The *Passions of the Soul*, though published in 1649, were composed two years earlier than the *Conversation*.)

CB 45. 1. 5. God made our body like a machine. For this famous Cartesian doctrine, see *Discourse*, Part V (AT vi. 56; HR i. 116). For 'machines' and 'mechanisms' in Cartesian science, see below on CB 73.

ll. 11/12. soul will be deceived. In the Sixth Meditation, Descartes lays great stress on the fact that the body is governed by the laws of physiology, in order to show that 'in spite of the immense goodness of God, it is of the nature of man compounded of mind and body that he cannot but be deceived on occasion' (AT vii. 88). Burman here raises an interesting objection to this defence; could God not have given the body some built-in 'warning mechanism' so as to put us on our guard when we were being fed misleading information? It is not at all clear from Descartes' reply why some kind of warning mechanism is impossible. And even if this is somehow ruled out by the requirement of 'uniform mechanical laws', why should not God benevolently intervene and implant in our minds some premonition of error when the senses provide misleading information?

CB 46 and 47. The problem about surfaces arose out of a theological objection by Arnauld in the Fourth Replies. Descartes denied the existence of secondary or sensible qualities (cf. above on CB 15); further, he held that the distinction between substance and attributes was not a 'real' one (cf. above on CB 36 and 22). Both these views, Arnauld objected, were inconsistent with the doctrine of the transubstantiation (AT vii. 217; HR ii. 95). Descartes replied, rather evasively, that his view of perception was that the *surface* (*superficies*) of an object acts on our senses; the Council of Trent decreed that in the Mass the appearance of the bread remains unchanged, and what was the appearance if not the surface? (AT vii. 251; HR ii. 118–19). Descartes defined 'surface' as the 'limit (*terminus*) which is conceived to lie between the single particles of a body and the bodies which surround it' (ibid.). But the authors of the Sixth Objections were unhappy about this, and raised the issue again.

By resurrecting the issue yet again, Burman (himself a Protestant) was perhaps trying to sound out the extent of Descartes' allegiance to Roman orthodoxy. But, true to form, Descartes steers clear of trouble. All he does is to slap the boards of the table at which they are sitting, thus given an ostensive definition of a 'flat surface' (CB 46, line 2).

At CB 47, Burman focuses on the notion of an extremity: in the Sixth Replies (loc. cit.) Descartes had said that although the surface was only a 'mode' and hence not *pars corporis* or *pars substantiae*, it could legitimately be called the *extremum corporis*. Picking up Descartes' remark that two bodies are contiguous when their extremities touch, Burman deploys an elaborate objection based on the scholastic distinction between *continuum* and *contiguum*. (As Adam notes at AT v. 164, the distinction is derived from Aristotle.) Can one properly talk of *contiguity*, Burman asks, when there are not really two extremities, but one? Compare *Principles* II, 15: 'per superficiem non hic intelligi ullam corporis . . . partem sed solum terminum . . .; vel certe intelligi superficiem in communi, quae non sit pars unius corporis magis quam alterius'. Once again, Descartes refuses to be drawn. His brusque remark at line 14 shows a characteristic contempt for the jargon of the Schools.

CB 47. ll. 17/18: which do not behave like this. For a more precise account of 'contiguity' (in connection with Descartes' denial of the possibility of a vacuum) see *Principles* II, 18 (AT viii. 50).

CB 48. This piece is unique in the *Conversation* in that it does not relate to a specific text. The opening word 'Observandum' introduces a general piece of advice which Descartes apparently launched into off his own bat. The point Descartes makes is important for its bearing on the vexed question of whether the chief driving force in Descartes' philosophy is metaphysical or scientific. (For a general discussion of this issue, see GIBSON, Ch. II.) On the face of it, the passage would seem to support the view of Adam, among others, that Cartesian metaphysics is merely a prologue to the science: '[Descartes] ne demande à la métaphysique qu'une chose, de fournir un appui solide à la vérité scientifique' (AT xii. 143). Certainly, the enthusiasm for physical science and its practical importance for life (lines 10 ff.) represents a serious and ongoing strand in Descartes' motivation: compare the *Discourse*, Part VI: 'au lieu de cete Philosophie spéculative, qu'on enseigne dans les escholes, on en peut trouver une pratique, par laquelle . . . nous . . . pourrions . . . nous rendre comme maistres et possesseurs de la Nature' (AT vi. 61–2; cf. AT i. 370). See also the striking personal revelation at CB 61, lines 36 ff.

l. 2. the *Meditations*. The small 'm' in the MS. should probably be emended to a capital; even if the small 'm' is correct, Descartes obviously has his own definitive statement of Metaphysics principally in mind (see line 13).

CB 49. This single piece deals with a passage from the *Notes against a Programme*. In the MS. the piece begins with the hieroglyph 'In R. ad Rog.'. *Rog.* (unemended in AT v., but corrected in Adam's special edition of the *Entretien*) should of course be *Prog.* Burman is referring to the reply ('R' = *Responsione*) to the anonymously circulated broadsheet of Regius, which had attacked certain of Descartes' doctrines on the nature of the mind.

The dispute with Regius was very much a hot issue at the time of the *Conversation* (April 1648). Regius' 'Programme', entitled 'The human mind or rational soul—an explanation of what it is and what it can be', had appeared only a few months previously ('sub. finem Anni 1647': AT viiib, *ad init.*). Descartes had written his reply at the end of December 1647, and it was published immediately—with rather precipitate haste, Descartes complains (AT v. 115)—under the title *Notae in programma quoddam*. Burman's reference is to this very recently published first edition ('p. 42' = AT viiib. 358). For Descartes' relations with Regius see below on CB 61. For the philosophical importance of his remarks here see Introduction, pp. xxxiv ff.

CB 50–75

The following twenty-six pieces take as their starting-points passages from the *Principles of Philosophy*; see Conspectus, pp. 123–5.

CB 50. ll. 9/10: not having been enacted and as alterable. Against Descartes' view that God must be thought of as 'accomplishing all things by means of a single act' (*per unicam actionem*, line 7), Burman raises the objection that some of God's decrees (e.g. that concerning the creation of the world) can theoretically be separated from him. His argument for the 'separability' of this decree is that God did not *have* to create the world, since it was completely in his power to do so or not—he was quite 'indifferent' (line 15). Thus the decree might not have been enacted—we can consider it as 'not having been enacted and as alterable' (tamquam non factum et mutabile)—and what God might not have done is not necessarily part of him.

l. 11. single act which is identical with God. The MS. is in need of slight restoration at this point. My translation follows this reconstruction: . . . 'quae ergo unica Dei actione *quae est* Deus non *fiant*, cum ab eo separari †non† possunt aut saltem potuerint'. This simply involves reading *quae est* where the original is indecipherable, and *fiant* for what looks like *fiat* (*sint*, Adam). This reconstruction seems to me preferable to Adam's, which involves rather more radical departures from the MS.; however, the general meaning is much the same. In any version the *non* in front of *possunt*, which was surely inserted by a slip of the copyist, should be deleted.

l. 37. Gomarists. One almost feels a shock of surprise that Descartes should be so incautious as to plump by name for one set of theologians against another. That he does so is a testimony to the relaxed and informal atmosphere which gives the *Conversation* its unique appeal. For details of the controversy referred to here see Introduction, pp. xxxvii ff.

CB 51. ll. 9/10: indefinite . . . infinite. The distinction between these two terms is Descartes' own (line 1), and he clearly regards it of some importance. It is referred to earlier in the *Conversation* (CB 21, q.v.) and, as well as in the passage quoted here from the *Principles*, it occurs frequently in the letters. Cf. letter to Chanut of June 1647: '. . . je ne dis pas que le monde soit infini, mais indéfini seulement. En quoi il y a une différence assez remarquable: car, pour dire qu'une chose est infinie, on doit avoir quelque raison qui la fasse connaître telle, ce qu'on ne peut avoir que de Dieu seul; mais pour dire qu'elle est indéfinie, il suffit de n'avoir point de raison par laquelle on puisse prouver qu'elle ait des bornes' (AT v. 51). '*X* is infinite', Descartes explains, can only be asserted on the strength of a conclusive reason; since he remarks that only in the case of God is a reason of the appropriate sort available, it would seem that he will only allow *X* to be called infinite if it can be logically demonstrated that *X* has no bounds. For the claim that *X* is indefinite, on the other hand, it is sufficient that we cannot prove that *X* has bounds—i.e. that it be logically possible that *X* is boundless.

The above account explains why Descartes in general talks of the physical universe as indefinite, rather than infinite. For it does not seem to be a necessary truth about the cosmos that it is limitless: we cannot in fact discern any limits, but there may be some. This is the implicit reasoning in lines 7–9 of CB 51. However, later on in the letter to Chanut, Descartes does sketch an argument to demonstrate the logical impossibility of a finite universe: '. . . in supposing the world to be finite, one imagines beyond its boundaries some spaces which are three-dimensional . . . [Yet since anything three-dimensional belongs in the universe] . . . this means that the universe must extend beyond the boundaries we tried to assign to it' (AT v. 52). Thus, for any circumference C assigned to the universe, it will always be possible to conceive of an area outside this circumference, which must then be included as part of the universe. And for the new circumference C_1 constructed to accommodate this additional area, an identical process of reasoning will apply. And so on. This argument is closely parallel to the proof that there is no largest natural number (for any allegedly largest number n, it will always be possible to conceive of a larger number $n + 1$, and so on); the type of self-repeating operation involved in this sort of reasoning was called by Descartes the 'multiplication of indefinites' (cf. CB 21, lines 15–21). Now the point about these arguments is that they do seem to show that it is (logically) impossible to talk of a largest number or (given that the universe is Euclidean) a bounded universe: so they would seem to license the use of the stricter term *infinite* for the series of numbers/the size of the universe. This seems to be what Descartes means when he says at CB 51 that 'when the indefinite is multiplied again and again . . . it is identical with infinity. So we can perhaps say that the world is infinite, and the same for number' (lines 10–13). In less informal situations, however, Descartes remained reluctant to apply the term 'infinite' to anything except God (cf. AT iii. 292; K 93); see More's criticism of his excessive caution in this matter (AT v. 242), and GIBSON, p. 248 for a probable explanation of it.

CB 52. The basic distinction made in the passage quoted from the *Principles* is between knowledge which involves extra-mental existence, and that which does not. Compare the more explicit French version: 'Je distingue tout ce qui tombe sous notre connaissance en deux genres: le premier contient toutes les choses qui ont quelque existence, et l'autre toutes les vérités qui ne sont rien hors de notre pensée' (AT ixb 45). Descartes now makes it clear to Burman that by 'eternal truths' he here has in mind none other than the common notions. 'Common notion' is used in Descartes more or less interchangeably with 'axiom' or 'common principle'; and Descartes has already pointed out earlier in the *Conversation* that these propositions have no relation to anything existing extra-mentally (see above on CB 1, line 26).

But is this all too neat and tidy? Referring to the passage at CB 52, A. Kenny makes the following observation: 'The expression "eternal truth" in the *Principles* is not a synonym of "axiom" as Descartes told Burman it was. If it were, he could not consistently have divided all possible objects of knowledge into things and eternal truths without denying that we could know any

non-axiomatic a priori truths' (KENNY (1), p. 178). This comment
is important for an assessment of the value of the *Conversation*
since it suggests that Descartes may have been inaccurate or careless when talking to Burman. But notice, first, that Descartes does
not use the word 'axiom' at all in this passage (though he does
use the virtually interchangeable term 'common notion': see
AT vii. 164, line 25). Second, Kenny fails to notice that what
Descartes says to Burman squares exactly with what he says later
on in the *Principles* when explaining his second category of objects
of knowledge (I, 49): a proposition in this category 'is to be
considered . . . as an eternal truth which has its seat in our mind,
and is called a common notion or axiom' (AT viii. 23). Third,
and most important, Descartes does not in any case say anything
about *synonymy*, either to Burman or in the *Principles*. At most, it
seems to me, identity of reference is implied here in CB 52.

It is of course true (not that Descartes denies it here) that the
connotation of 'eternal verity' is different from that of 'axiom or
common notion'. *Eternal* truths, as their name suggests, are un-
changeable—true for all time (éternelles et immuables; AT i. 146).
The main fact about them stated in the *Principles* is that they do
not involve extra-mental existence. And now all Descartes need
be taken to be pointing out to Burman is that what he had in
mind as meeting these criteria of unchanging truth and lack of
existential import were the axioms or common notions.

But are the axioms the only propositions to meet the criteria?
Here it seems to me that Kenny is quite right to point out that
there must be the possibility of non-axiomatic eternal verities in
Descartes' system (e.g. mathematical theorems). But the dis-
tinction between axiom and theorem (important though it is from
the point of view of immediate self-evidence) is one which
Descartes is inclined to blur. Some of the 'axioms' listed in the
Second Replies are quite complex to state, and as Descartes him-
self admits, they might better have been demonstrated as theorems
(AT vii. 164).

**ll. 6/7. Contingent truths involve existing things, and vice
versa.** If the distinction between eternal and contingent corresponds with that between propositions carrying no existential
import and those which do, is not Descartes moving remarkably
close to a Humean position on scientific truth? Will not physical
science, since it deals with existing things, have to be of a contingent character? And if this is so, what becomes of the 'deduct-
ivist' or 'aprioristic' view of natural science with which Descartes
is so often credited?

I think part of the answer is that in so far as the laws of science
are, for Descartes, eternal verities, they deal with relations between

essences; the propositions involved are thus not of an existential character. In this respect they are closely parallel to (indeed often *are*) mathematical propositions; and these, as Descartes tells us, do not require actual existence for their truth. The difference between mathematics and physics is not in the character of the laws studied, but merely that the physicist introduces the (contingent) assertion that the objects which he is studying are to be regarded as actually existing. This is explained very clearly at CB 34, lines 9–19 q.v. When this has been said, however, one can, I think, greatly exaggerate the extent to which Cartesian science is *simply* a matter of the *a priori* deduction of eternal verities: see below on CB 74, line 2.

CB 53. ll. 6/7: what we 'see' must ultimately reduce to what 'appears' to us. It is merely ideas that are, for Descartes, the proper objects of immediate perception (Sixth Meditation, AT vii. 75, line 7; cf. vii. 436–7); hence 'anyone is capable of denying' that these originate in extended physical objects. ('Anyone' of course includes Descartes himself in the mood of the First Meditation.) In saying that these appearances in fact 'require' or 'demand' (*exigere*) the existence of material objects as their source (line 8), Descartes is assuming the already proved existence of a non-deceiving God, a point made explicitly both in the paragraph of the *Principles* referred to here and in the corresponding part of the Sixth Meditation (AT vii. 80; HR i. 191).

CB 54. To think that more activity is needed for motion than for rest is a prejudice, Descartes argues, derived from our human experience: it is an 'effort' to move our bodies when we are tired, and we take this as the model for our view of the causality of motion. The illustration of the ship, which needs as great a force to stop it as to set it going (except for the qualification explained here to Burman), is given by Descartes as an aid for ridding ourselves of this prejudice.

l. 5. 'viscosity'. Adam suggests (AT ixb. 77) that this must be what is meant by the rather vague Latin word *lentor*. (The French version of the *Principles* simply renders this as 'lenteur'.) For some interesting conceptual problems in fitting a notion like 'viscosity' into the framework of Cartesian physics, see WILLIAMS, p. 352.

CB 55. The point made 'at the end of the section' (line 5) is that, even though 'absolutely speaking' one should speak only of a single motion in a given body, it may often be useful to distinguish various components (e.g. the rectilinear and circular motion of the carriage wheel).

CB 56. These few lines are valuable evidence on the question of

Descartes' contribution to the French version of the *Principles*. This version ('Les Principes de la Philosophie, escrits en Latin par René Des Cartes et Traduits en François par un de ses Amis') was published in Paris by Henri le Gras in 1647. The 'friend' referred to is known to be the Abbé Picot. Now this edition contains a considerable number of substantial additions and modifications to the original Latin version, which it is hard to believe that Picot would have ventured to supply on his own initiative (compare, e.g. the two versions of II, 49–51). The possibility that the additions are Descartes' own work is suggested by the inventory of his papers which was made at Stockholm just after he died; this contains the item: 'soixante & neuf feuillets . . . contenant la doctrine de ses Principes en françois & non entirement conformes a l'imprimé latin'. Handwritten notes in two extant copies of the first French edition give further support for Descartes' own authorship of certain passages. (This evidence is cited in detail in AT ixb.: *Avertissement*.) But here in the *Conversation*, we have proof 'straight from the author' that Descartes did make additions of his own. And although the comment to Burman refers only to the rules on movement in Book II, the strong inference must be that the other substantial additions, or at least the bulk of them, are Descartes' own work.

The reason for Descartes' additions was not that he was dissatisfied with Picot's version (he speaks of it in flattering terms when writing to Picot in February 1645: AT iv. 181); rather, as is made clear here at CB 56, Descartes took the opportunity of a second edition to enlarge upon and clarify certain passages which had caused trouble to readers of the original Latin edition. The comment that 'many were complaining' of the obscurity of the 'laws' (the seven rules for determining the subsequent motions of colliding bodies: Articles 46–52) is confirmed in a letter to Clerselier (17 February 1645), where Descartes promises 'je tascherois de les [ces regles] eclaircir d'avantage . . .' (AT iv. 187).

CB 57. l. 3: for their benefit. This notion is associated with the search for final causes which Descartes utterly rejects (cf. on CB 29). See also CB 65: we mistakenly think of the earth as the 'end of all things' (*finis omnium*); but it is really just an ordinary planet like Mars and Saturn (lines 6 ff.). In the *Principles*, Descartes concedes that the anthropocentric view, though absurd for science, may be acceptable in the ethical sphere (to say that all things were made by God for our sake may impel us to give thanks and burn with love for him: AT viii. 81). But here in the *Conversation*, even this let-out seems closed. For if there may be an infinite number of creatures 'far superior to us' (line 20), then the privileged place of man in God's plan seems threatened; and this has obvious implications from the ethical and religious standpoint (cf. the letter to Chanut of June 1647, AT v. 55). Descartes is seldom as frank about the implications of the new cosmology as he is here (and in the following piece on Genesis); and though God stays very much in the picture (lines 12 ff.) his purposes remain firmly hidden in a way which foreshadows the deistic movements of the following century. (For a discussion of the ethical implications of a cosmos of innumerable 'worlds', cf. Leibniz, *Theodicy*, Bk. I, § 19.)

CB 58. Descartes had long hoped to provide a detailed reconciliation between his own theory of the origin of the world and the account in Genesis. In 1641 he had told Mersenne that he intended to send the Sorbonne an explanation, based on his own scientific principles, of the first book of Genesis and of the transubstantiation (AT iii. 295). Here, however (esp. lines 3–6), we see how exasperating for Descartes this task turned out to be. The obvious stumbling-block with the reconciliation project is that Descartes' whole aim is, in effect, to describe the gradual evolution of the cosmos from prime elements in accordance with scientific laws, rather than accepting a creation of the ready-made variety. The basic thrust of his 'mechanistic' philosophy is to search for the origins of complex phenomena in terms of their emergence from the interaction of primitive particles which operate on simple 'mechanical' laws (cf. below on CB 73). This means that understanding an object as it is now is intimately tied up with understanding its causal development—a point which Descartes explicitly makes later on in the *Conversation*: one cannot explain the functions of an animal without having to explain its formation right back *ab ovo* (CB 61, lines 26/8). To avoid an open clash with the theologians, Descartes had taken the frequent let-out of suggesting that his own account was only a 'hypothesis', while the biblical story was 'much more probable' (see *Discourse*, Part V (AT vi. 48); *Principles* III, 44–5 (AT viii. 100); and cf. GILSON (2), pp. 380–1 and COLLINS, pp. 7 ff.).

ll. 15/17. Augustine . . . thoughts of the angels. Augustine, arguing that the six 'days' of Genesis Chapter 1 cannot be taken literally (since the sun was not created till the fourth 'day'), had given a completely mystical and metaphorical interpretation of the six-day creation. His thesis was that the 'morning and evening' composing each day (Gen. 1:5 etc.) are to be interpreted as referring to two phases in the thoughts of the angels—their 'morning' and 'evening' thoughts (cognitio matutina et verspertina; see *De Gen. ad Litt.*, Book IV, esp. Ch. 41 (xxiv) ff.).

ll. 18/20. waters of the flood (*aquae diluvii*) . . . cataracts of the deep (*cataractae abyssi*). A reference to the story of Noah and the flood: 'ego adducam aquas diluvii super terram' (Gen. 6:17); 'et clausi sunt fontes abyssi et cataractae caeli' (Gen. 8:2). Descartes' own view of the story is summed up by the words 'supernatural', 'miraculous', and 'metaphorical' (lines 19/20). But at lines 21 ff., we have a brief glimpse into his earlier (abandoned) attempt to provide an account of Genesis consistent with his own philosophy. It is interesting to see that Descartes took this project seriously enough to tackle the original Hebrew; but, if what is offered to Burman is any guide, his studies were not too successful (see below).

l. 24. placed the waters above *ha shamayim*. In Genesis 1:1–6, God creates the 'firmament of heaven' which divides the waters above from those below. Descartes' suggestion seems to be that we should demystify the phrase 'waters above the heaven', and realize that it means merely 'waters above the air', or clouds. But the alleged ambiguity in the Hebrew on which his argument turns is just not there: as Adam points out (AT v. 169) *ha shamayim* only means 'the heavens', never 'the air'.

l. 28. another word. This seems to be a straight mistake: *ha aretz* can only mean 'the earth'. Adam suggests that the Hebrew word in the MS. should perhaps be amended to read *ha aver* (the air); although this is a borrowed Greek word which does not occur in biblical Hebrew.

CB 59. Descartes' second law of motion is that 'any given piece of matter considered in itself tends to go on moving in a straight line'. But Descartes also maintains that the net result of the *collision* of innumerable particles must always be a circular motion. The details of the argument referred to here may be found at AT viii. 58–9.

CB 60. ll. 1/2. first element. Descartes' 'three elements' are described in article 52 of *Principles* III. In effect these are merely classifications of the single basic material of the universe with respect to shape and magnitude. The first element, out of which the sun and 'fixed stars' are formed, comprises high-speed particles which divide into indefinitely small fragments. The 'thicker' particles of the third element are those from which the earth and planets (and the comets) are formed. The particles of the second element, whose size Descartes here describes, are those which compose the heavens (cf. AT viii. 105).

CB 61. ll. 2 and 9 ff. Regius. Regius, or Henri le Roy (1598–1679), a native of Utrecht and Professor of Theoretical Medicine and Botany at the University there, was for some years a great champion of the Cartesian philosophy. His *Fundamenta Physica* (which Burman has in mind at line 2) was published in 1646. Descartes complained to Mersenne that much of the book was a repetition of things he himself had said in the *Principles, Dioptrics*, and *Meteors* (AT iv. 510; K 204). But what evidently irritated Descartes even more than the plagiarism and confusion in matters of physics was that Regius had put forward metaphysical views diametrically opposed to his own (lines 13 ff.). These metaphysical differences had led Descartes to insert a sharp disavowal of Regius' views in the Preface to the French edition of the *Principles* (AT ixb. 19). Regius had, for example, put forward two thoroughly uncartesian theses regarding the nature of the mind and human knowledge: 'mens est principium corporeum'; and 'nihil scimus nisi secundum apparentiam' (AT iv. 566). See also above on CB 49.

l. 18. confirms the hypothesis. See below on CB 74, line 2.

ll. 24/5. Treatise on the Animal. It was a long-standing project of Descartes to write a treatise on animal anatomy and physiology. See the letter to Elizabeth of January 1648: 'j'ai maintenant un autre écrit entre les mains . . .: c'est la description des fonctions de l'animal et de l'homme. Car ce que j'en avais brouillé, il y a douze ou treize ans, qui a été vu par Votre Altesse, étant venu entre les mains de plusieurs qui l'ont mal transcrit, j'ai crû être obligé de le mettre plus au net, c'est a dire de le refaire' (AT v. 122; cf. AT iv. 310). As we see from lines 34 ff., however, Descartes had abandoned the rewriting project by the following April. Evidently, the plan of 'tidying up' the work turned out to require a more lengthy treatment than Descartes felt prepared to give at this time; and the book was never in fact completed.

CB 62–64. These all relate to the same passage, though in the original MS. the piece which I number CB 63 is placed after CB 71, at the end of the pieces relating to Book III of the *Principles*; presumably it was inadvertently omitted by the copyist, and then simply inserted later on, when he paused to check the pieces relating to Book III. A similar mispositioning occurs at CB 36.

The reference at the end of CB 62 is to *Principles* III, 122/3. At the end of CB 63, the original Latin, as quite often, is completely unpunctuated. I follow the text in ADAM: 'habebimus superficies multo plures; multo plures si longe plus multiplicantur ab omni parte'.

At CB 64 Descartes makes the point that in distinguishing mass from surface he is not implying that they are *in reality* distinct: the distinction is purely theoretical (cf. above on CB 36). For the phrase 'theoretical notion' (*ratio formalis*, line 3) cf. AT vii. 113, where Descartes says that in speaking about the infinite one may either talk in terms of a purely theoretical notion or definition (ratio formalis infiniti, sive infinitas), or one may talk of a real thing which is infinite (res quae est infinita).

CB 65. Descartes' 'first heaven' is the vortex which makes up the local solar system, with our sun in the centre. The 'second heaven' consists of the vast number of vortexes centred around the other fixed stars. Stretching beyond the visible stars is the 'third heaven'. By using the term 'empyrean' to Burman (line 1) Descartes merely means that his *tertium caelum* may be thought of as corresponding to the 'highest heaven' of medieval cosmology (whose ancestor was the outermost 'fiery sphere' of the Greeks). Though Descartes does say piously that it is impossible for us to view the third heaven 'in this life' (AT vii. 107), we can see from lines 8 ff. here that he is not reverting to the traditional view of the empyrean as the dwelling-place of God and the angels. The main scientific importance of a *tertium caelum* is that it affirms the existence of an indefinitely extended cosmos (cf. above on CB 51).
1. 10. neither space. Matter and extension are identical for Descartes, since there can be no extension which is not extension of *something*: hence Descartes regards the notion of a vacuum as incoherent; see *Principles* II, 18 (AT viii. 50).
ll. 12/13. could not but be present. But exactly how an unextended indivisible God can be 'present' in extended divisible matter is not clear (cf. above on CB 43).

CB 67. Quotation: There is no Latin quotation here in the MS.; Burman simply identifies the relevant passage by the article number.
1. 1. this figure. This is reproduced at AT viii. 118 (see note ad loc.). For Descartes' pride in the way he has trained his powers of imagination cf. CB 42, lines 30 ff.
1. 7. visual demonstration. The mathematician needs great powers of visualization (or, failing that, an actual visual demonstration using a model); see further, on CB 79. For the linking of 'mathematics' and 'mechanics' see below on CB 73, line 3.

CB 68–71: four technical pieces dealing with Descartes' theories of motion. Burman's question at CB 68 seems a reasonable one; but Descartes acknowledges no interstellar 'space' (see above on CB 65). It follows that where one vortex ends, another begins. The figure referred to at CB 69 may be found at AT viii. 88. The point about *constriction* is illustrated by a neat mechanical model which is reproduced at AT viii. 138.

In one way, the top analogy at CB 70 suggests a universe which is slowly running down. The top suffers a gradual loss of momentum, owing (as Descartes explains to Burman) to factors like friction and air resistance; and analogous factors must, for Descartes, operate on the stellar and planetary scale. However, the effects of friction etc. are—especially in the case of a massive body (lines 6–10)—very marginal, so that the universe, once set in motion, has more than enough momentum to keep it going to the present day without any additional forces. So the point which Descartes is really making here is that the universe is—very nearly—in a state of equilibrium (cf. CB 73). Elsewhere, though (perhaps out of caution), Descartes does seem to want to assert that the continuous agency of God is necessary in order to conserve motion (see letter to More, AT v. 404; K 258).

At CB 71, Descartes is apparently thinking of the sort of thing that happens when one blows up a balloon; the point of the comparison is simply to illustrate how an object can be acted upon by forces from within. The explanation of the rotation of the earth accords with Descartes' theory of the origin of the planets; according to this, the planets were originally quasi-stellar objects, each at the centre of its own vortex (see *Principles* III, 119 and 146).

CB 72. l. 15: make them heavy. Descartes' theory of gravity may nowadays seem to be nothing more than a curiosity in the history of science; but at least it rejects the non-solution of attributing to bodies a mysterious 'real quality' of *gravitas*. See further, on CB 73.

CB 73. l. 3: mathematical and mechanical (*mathematicum et mechanicum*). The two terms are to be taken closely together; a similar coupling occurs at CB 67, lines 5/6 (haec a mathesi et mechanica pendent). The most precise statement of what Descartes means by 'mechanics' occurs in a letter to Plempius (3 October 1637), where Descartes says that his philosophy, 'like mechanics, considers shapes, sizes, and motions' (AT i. 420; K 38). Exactly what this involves can be seen in the case of gravity (referred to at CB 72). The phenomenon is explained simply in terms of the interaction of particles of a certain shape, size, and velocity; no reference is made to 'real qualities'. The tie-up between mathematics and mechanics would thus seem to be this: Cartesian science deals only with the shape, size, and motion of particles; since these are exactly quantifiable, the laws determining the interaction of the particles will be suitable for description by means of precise mathematical formulae. As Descartes himself says in a famous passage from the *Principles*: 'I recognize no other matter in corporeal objects than that susceptible of what the Geometers call quantitative analysis of divisions, shapes, and motions . . .' (II, 64).

But if we look at how Descartes' programme works out *in practice*, the 'mechanical' element becomes more important, and the mathematical element less important, than this general account suggests. In the *Conversation*—here at CB 73, and at CB 67—Descartes lays great stress on what we should nowadays call *mechanical models*. At CB 67, he points out that the movements involved in the vortexes can only be understood with reference to the model of the 'little balls' (without this, he says, it is not really possible to understand even the diagram in the *Principles*). And at CB 73, the equilibrium of the particles of celestial matter is explained by reference to the model of the bladder, or balloon. Now one could argue that these models are purely illustrative; this is certainly part of their function, since the model in CB 67 is described as an aid to imagination. But there seems to be more to it than this, for at CB 73, after saying that the point about equilibrium is 'mathematical and mechanical', Descartes goes on to make the following very striking observation (lines 3-5): 'nos autem machinas non satis asseuti sumus considerare et hinc omnis fere error in philosophia exorsus est' (we are not sufficiently accustomed to thinking of machines, and this has been the source of nearly all error in philosophy [i.e. science]). This suggests that the mechanical model has a central role in Cartesian science; what this role is emerges, I believe, out of Descartes' conception of scientific explanation. Descartes' scientific explanations are not simply mathematical laws; indeed, it is striking that there are almost no equations, or arithmetical or algebraic formulae in the *Principles* (an exception are the rules for determining the motions of bodies on impact, *Principles* II, 46-52). Descartes himself observes at CB 79 that 'you do not . . . need Mathematics to understand the author's philosophical [i.e. scientific] writings, with the possible exception of a few mathematical points in the *Dioptrics*' (lines 23 ff.). What we do find, over and over again in the *Principles*, are little diagrams, generally representing models—arrangements of little balls in boxes and the like. This strongly suggests that Descartes regards the scientist's role as that of making phenomena intelligible by providing a model which explains the *mechanism* by which the basic laws operate. For this conception compare the following quotation:

The proper use of models is the basis of scientific thinking . . . Our lack of knowledge of the real mechanisms at work in nature is supplemented by our imagining something analogous to mechanisms which we know, which could perhaps exist in nature and be responsible for the phenomena we observe. Such imagined mechanisms are models, modelled *on* the things and processes we know, and being models *of* the unknown processes and things which are responsible for the phenomena which we are studying. (HARRÉ, pp. 174-5)

I do not of course suggest that Descartes' views of the role of the model in scientific explanation are as developed or detailed as this. Nevertheless accounts of Descartes' 'mechanism' which confine themselves to the elimination of real qualities in favour of quantifiables and fail to notice the specific importance of mechanical models do seem crucially deficient. (Cf. P. H. J. Hoenen, *Descartes's Mechanism*, printed in DONEY (1), pp. 353-68; and KENNY (1), pp. 203 ff.)

CB 74. l. 2: reasoning . . . experience. The orthodox view of Cartesian science is that it rejects empirical experiment in favour of rigid *a priori* deductivism (cf. GIBSON, p. 183; KENNY (1), pp. 206 and 213). Descartes' attempts in the *Principles* to deduce the laws of motion from the nature of God (AT viii. 61 ff.) certainly provide strong support for this interpretation. But the comment here at CB 74 suggests a more subtle conception, more akin to the 'hypothetico-deductive' model of science. The vital confirmatory role of experiment is also stressed in the letter to Plempius for Fromondus of 3 October 1637 (AT i. 421; K 38) as well as in the *Discourse* (AT vi. 64-5; HR i. 121) and the *Principles* (AT viii. 101). Notice too the passage at CB 61, where Descartes talks of his vortex theory as a hypothesis which has been confirmed by the large number of consequences deduced from it (lines 16/17). Two further points in this interesting passage suggest a far more sophisticated scientific methodology than the caricature of armchair apriorism. First, the notion of explanatory *simplicity* plays a key role in Descartes' thinking: his object is to subsume as wide a variety as possible of diverse phenomena under a sparse and economical covering principle (lines 15-19). Second, Descartes shows a complete grasp of the importance of the *scope* of a scientific theory. It is no great achievement to construct, *post hoc*, a covering law for a finite range of phenomena. What Descartes (in common with scientists today) takes to be a striking consideration in favour of a theory is that its scope can be extended to cover a wider range of phenomena, and even different *kinds* of phenomena, than those which it was originally designed to account for (see lines 19-24).

l. 4. shapes in question. The three kinds of particles referred to are (1) 'branching'; (2) solid and angular, like pebbles of various shapes; (3) oblong, like a stick. There is a discussion of some of the alleged observational evidence for Descartes' classification in the letter to Plempius for Fromondus referred to above (AT i. 422–3; K 39–40).

CB 75. Descartes' explanation of the formation of glass. Nine articles in the *Principles* (IV, 124–32) are devoted to this; and we know from the *Discourse* (AT vi. 44–5) that a (now missing) section of *Le Monde* had also dealt with the topic.

l. 24. Book Two. See Article 63: 'Why some bodies are so hard that despite their small size they cannot easily be divided by our hands' (AT viii. 77).

CB 76–82

This concluding section of the *Conversation* consists of seven pieces dealing with points from the *Discourse*. Burman's quotations are not from the first edition of the *Discourse*, but from the 1644 Latin translation; accordingly, my translation of the quotations is based on this Latin version (to be found at the end of AT vi.). The page references which I have supplied after each quotation are to AT's Latin text; but for convenience I have added, in brackets, a reference to the corresponding page of the AT French text. Thus, the quotation at CB 76 may be found in AT vi, page 540 (Latin) or pages 1 and 2 (French).

CB 76. l. 9. 'good sense'. In the *Discourse*, *le bon sens* (translated in the Latin version as 'bona mens') is defined as the 'power of distinguishing the true from the false' (AT vi. 2). In the opening sentence of the *Discourse* Descartes claims it is the 'most equally distributed thing in the world', and is 'naturally equal in all men'. Burman's objection to this surprisingly egalitarian thesis (lines 1/2) seems very apposite; for Descartes himself admits in the *Discourse* that he has often wished he was as well endowed with powers of thought (la pensée), imagination, or memory as some of his acquaintances, adding that these three faculties are the only ones he knows of that contribute to perfection of mind (AT vi. 2, lines 20–6).

The logic of Descartes' reply to Burman (lines 5/7) is bizarre: the fact that everyone *thinks* his judgement is good does not of course entail that it *is* good. More puzzling still is the comment at lines 7/8: everyone is happy with his own views, and to 'no two think alike' (quot capita tot sensus; a variant of the Terentian tag 'quot homines tot sententiae'). It seems just tendentious for Descartes to go on to say that this is what he meant by good sense (line 9). 'No you did not!', one feels tempted to reply on Burman's behalf; 'in the *Discourse* you talked of a "power to judge well and distinguish the true from the false", which is something completely different'.[1]

A possible defence of Descartes is that when he talks of 'la puissance de distinguer le vrai d'avec le faux', he has in mind a potentiality, rather than an ability which is actualized in all of us. The Latin version of the *Discourse* makes this clearer by talking of a power which is 'naturally equal and inborn in all of us' (vim natura aequalem omnibus nobis innatam; AT vi. 540, line 8). This innate faculty will not automatically produce correct opinions (indeed, Descartes' whole method supposes the existence of 'prejudices' which need critical scrutiny); it needs, if truth is to be attained, to be *applied* correctly, i.e. methodically and with concentration. Elsewhere, instead of 'sense' or 'reason' (le sens; la raison), Descartes uses the more familiar metaphor of the 'light of reason' or the 'natural light' (la lumière naturelle); and he observes to Mersenne: 'since all men have the same natural light, it seems that they should all have the same notions; this is far from the case, because there is hardly anyone who makes good use of this light, so that many people—e.g. everyone of our acquaintance—may agree in making the same mistake' (16 October 1639; AT ii. 598; K 66).

CB 77. ll. 1/2: Logic . . . Dialectic. In the section of the *Discourse* referred to here, Descartes makes his famous attack on the traditional logic of the Schools. (For the reference to the 'art of Lully' in the passage quoted, see GILSON (2), pp. 185–6.) Descartes' objection, as we see here, is not to formal logic *per se*, but to 'Dialectic', viz. the prevailing method of study which restricted its application to 'stock arguments and headings' (lines 5/6). See further *Regulae* X, AT x. 405–6.

l. 8. Professor Voetius. The original Latin has 'Dn. [i.e. Dominus] Voetius'. 'Professor', as used in modern English, seems the nearest equivalent to this respectful prefix with its academic flavour. The respect, in Descartes' case, is of course heavily ironical.

Gisbertus Voetius (1589–1676), one of Descartes' most implacable opponents, was Professor of Theology at the University of Utrecht, and was elected Rector there in 1641. In that year he,

---

[1] Gilson, noting a close parallel between the first sentence of the *Discourse* and a passage in Montaigne's *Essay on Presumption*, suggests that the opening of the *Discourse* may contain 'une nuance d'ironie' (GILSON (2), p. 83). The tone of the remarks here to Burman certainly supports this view. But Descartes' irony should presumably illustrate, or at least not contradict, the serious thesis which he wishes to advance concerning the equal distribution of good sense. So we still have to explain the relation between Everyman's proverbial satisfaction in his powers of judgement, and the serious thesis.

and his son Paul, also a professor at Utrecht, mounted a bitter attack on the Cartesian philosophy then being expounded at Utrecht by Regius (see above on CB 61). The brunt of the attack was theological—Cartesian 'scepticism' was held up as anti-religious and a danger to faith. Eventually, Voetius succeeded in getting the university senate to ban all teaching of Descartes' philosophy. For Descartes' counter-attack, see the *Épître au Père Dinet* (1642); the *Epistula ad Voetium* (May 1643); and the 'Lettre Apologétique'—'A letter in self-defence written to the Magistrates of Utrecht against the two Voetii, father and son' (July 1643). (For an account of the 'Utrecht Controversy' see VROOMAN, pp. 156–65.)

CB 78. 1. 1. Theology. The *Conversation* is a valuable source for Descartes' attitude to theology and theologians. In the correspondence, notably in the letters to Mersenne, Descartes comes across as anxious to steer clear of difficult theological issues (e.g. the Trinity—AT iii. 374; eternal damnation—AT i. 158). In the *Conversation*, when Burman raises a theological question, Descartes frequently distinguishes between the job of the 'philosopher' and that of the 'theologian': questions to be left to the latter include grace and salvation (CB 32); prelapsarian immortality (CB 82); and the interpretation of the creation story (CB 58).

Here at CB 78, Burman wants to know how Descartes can justify this syphoning off of religious questions to the sphere of theology in view of the famous Cartesian doctrine of the interconnectedness of all knowledge (stated in the passage quoted from the *Discourse*). In Descartes' reply, three points about theological truths emerge. First, their derivation is greatly more complex than in the case of philosophy; we cannot follow the various connections in the same way (line 6). Second, by 'Theology', as distinct from 'Philosophy', Descartes means the investigation of the *revealed* truths of religion (line 5; i.e. those which depend on scripture and the teachings of the Church). Questions about the existence of God and the immortality of the soul, on the other hand, are described by Descartes as 'praecipuae ex iis quae Philosophiae potius quam Theologiae ope sunt demonstrandae' (*Meditations*: Dedicatory Letter, AT vii. 1). Thirdly, although the truths of revealed theology are not to be critically examined, the philosopher must at least be sure that they are not inconsistent with his results (lines 13–15). This remark explains certain departures from Descartes' stated policy of 'leaving it to the theologians' which would otherwise be puzzling (see above on CB 46–7 and CB 58).

In the second half of CB 78 we see a more personal motive for

Descartes' reluctance to become embroiled in theological issues. Throughout his life, Descartes was plagued by critics who were ready to claim that his aim was to 'subvert religion and faith' (CB 80). The principal target at which Descartes bitterly lashes out at lines 16 ff. is the 'monks' and their 'scholastic theology' (i.e. the Thomist tradition in which Descartes had been well grounded at La Flèche). In place of this Descartes proposes a simple theology like that of the ignorant 'country folk' (*rustici*, line 24), which, he notes, is quite sufficient for salvation. This picks up a phrase in the *Discourse*: 'le chemin [au ciel] n'en est pas moins ouvert aux plus ignorants qu'aux plus doctes' (AT vi. 8; see further GILSON (2), pp. 132 ff.).

Descartes' preference for a 'reformed' theology perhaps explains in part his decision to settle in Holland for most of his life. The question of a religious motive for emigration is considered by Professor Vrooman in his biography of Descartes, but summarily rejected: 'what need was there for a Catholic in France to fear persecution?' (VROOMAN, p. 75). But there are many forms of persecution, and Descartes' complaints here against the 'abuse' of his philosophy show that Vrooman's argument is a great deal too swift. But whatever Descartes' motives, he certainly did not find the Protestant professors of theology any closer to his ideal. And when he talks at the end of CB 78 of theologians who are adept at 'foisting views on their opponents and denigrating them' (lines 27 ff.), it seems that he has broadened his attack and has in mind the professors of Utrecht as much as anyone (cf. above on CB 77, line 7).

CB 79. ll. 9/10: no books with him. The period referred to is that described in Part II of the *Discourse*, i.e. the winter of 1619 which Descartes spent in Bavaria, closeted in his famous 'stove-heated room' (AT vi. 11).

l. 14. Algebra. Descartes is thinking in particular of a system for correlating numerical and spatial relations, which had been one of his earliest preoccupations (cf. correspondence with Beeckman: AT x. 156–7). In Part II of the *Discourse*, Descartes explains how, for the purpose of dealing with several simultaneous (geometrical) relations, he decided that he had best use 'quelques chiffres les plus courts qu'il serait possible' (AT vi. 20 and 551; see also AT xii. 52–4, for Descartes' pioneering work in this field).

l. 19. a certain Frenchman. Adam suggests, plausibly, that the reference must be to the French mathematician Debeaune. Florimond Debeaune (1601–52) had worked through Descartes' *Geometry* and written an introduction and explanatory notes. Descartes had corresponded with Debeaune and seen his work;

when van Schooten published his Latin version of the *Geometry*, Descartes asked him to include Debeaune's material. This impending publication was uppermost in Descartes' mind at the time of the *Conversation*. A few days before meeting Burman, he wrote to Mersenne about it (AT v. 143). Schooten (Frans van Schooten the Younger) was Professor of Mathematics at Leyden University from 1646; so it is likely that Burman, himself from Leyden (see Introduction), would know about his forthcoming version of the *Geometry*, and would pick up the reference to Debeaune.

ll. 41/2. no place for imagination. By 'imagination' Descartes means, quite literally, the act of forming an image, or 'visualizing', as opposed to 'pure understanding' (see above on CB 21). Yet this makes the comment about physics, and the contrast with mathematics, rather odd; one might have expected just the opposite, since it is mathematics which seems, *par excellence*, a subject for 'pura intellectio'. Yet in a letter to Elizabeth, Descartes repeats that mathematical objects '*can* be known by understanding alone, but much better when aided by imagination' (AT iii. 691–2; K 141. See further *Regulae* XIV, AT x. 438 ff. and BECK, pp. 215 ff.). But if it is a matter of the imagination *aiding* the intellect, why cannot this happen in physics? To add to the puzzle, Descartes remarks elsewhere, this time to Mersenne, that imagination is equally inappropriate when it comes to metaphysics: 'la partie de l'esprit qui aide le plus aux Mathématiques, à savoir, l'imagination, nuit plus qu'elle ne sert pour les Spéculations Metaphysiques' (AT ii. 622).

The explanation of these comments is, I think, this. Imagination, as Descartes explains at CB 42, is closely allied to perception. Both involve the depiction of images in the brain—the only difference is that in imagination the job is done 'with the windows shut' (line 19). Now the sensory images of perception are closely tied up with the false beliefs and prejudices which the metaphysician needs to disregard in his search after truth (cf. *Meditation* I); similarly, the physicist needs to avoid attributing to matter the 'real qualities' which his senses have led him to believe in (cf. CB 15). Thus, the formation of images which we may be tempted to foist on the world of reality can be, for Descartes, a source of disastrous error in metaphysics and physics. In mathematics, on the other hand, there is no question of the objects of study 'really existing'; mathematical entities are considered merely as possibles (CB 34). Thus the image is a help to the mathematical student in marshalling his thoughts, rather than a tempting picture of reality.

However, even if this account is correct, in view of the fact that mathematical theorems can be applied to physics Descartes' categorical assertion that physics has 'no place' for imagination seems too strong; indeed, it is inconsistent with his own comment at CB 67 that the actual visible model (as a substitute for imagination) can be vital for grasping a 'mathematical and mechanical' point in physics. To rescue Descartes here, we should perhaps make a distinction between the heuristic and expository roles of the physicist: perhaps Descartes means that it is in discovering new truths that the imagination may be treacherous; in explaining a theory once arrived at, visualization and the use of models is a valuable bonus.

l. 61. more solid proof. Why are the proofs of metaphysics more solid than those of mathematics? Apparently because they can be established in the teeth of the radical doubts of the *Meditations*, while mathematical proofs cannot (lines 62–6). This is odd, because in the *Meditations* '2 + 3 = 5' seems to rank *pari passu* with 'cogito ergo sum' as indubitably true despite the most extreme doubts (AT vii. 36; HR i. 158). Similarly, Descartes admits that the atheist (i.e. one who lacks any metaphysical guarantee of a non-deceiving God) can know that the angles of a triangle equal two right angles (AT vii. 141; HR i. 39).

The way out of this, I think, is that the truths just mentioned are of an extremely simple nature ('2 + 3 = 5' is 'aliquid valde simplex et facile': AT vii. 36); they can therefore be known for certain, since everything relevant to their truth can be simultaneously present and open to the attentive mind. When Descartes says at CB 79 that in the face of extreme metaphysical doubts 'absolutely no mathematical proof could be given with certainty', he must be thinking of more complex pieces of reasoning which are too elaborate to be grasped by the mind in their entirety. In the case of these elaborate proofs—the 'longues chaînes de raisons' characteristic of mathematics—we are dealing with a whole system of interconnected logical relations, and here a finite mind can make no progress without first establishing the metaphysical premiss of a non-deceiving God. This can be established 'in spite of the doubt' (line 66) because we are able to grasp the proof of God's existence in its entirety. (CB 6, line 52; cf. Introduction, p. xxxi.)

CB 80. These few lines provide a fascinating insight into both the writing of the *Discourse* and Descartes' general attitude to ethics. But the one commentator who has noticed the importance of the lines seems anxious to qualify their impact. In his Commentary on the *Discourse* Gilson observes that the lines from the *Conversation* may not strictly reflect Descartes' attitude when writing the *Discourse* (over ten years earlier): Descartes might be 'projecting back' the caution he had learnt as a result of the bitter attacks he had suffered during the forties. However, Descartes does specifically say that his motive *for including the rules* was to avoid the calumny of the Schoolmen; he is thus quite clearly referring to the time of writing. Is it really plausible to suppose that he had forgotten his own state of mind when preparing this most carefully planned introduction to his work—the first book he agreed to publish? Further, though Descartes had suffered a lot from calumny in the forties, he was just as conscious of the need for caution in the previous decade; the suppression of *Le Monde*, after all, was in 1634.

l. 3. Schoolmen. For Descartes' difficulties at the hands of academic theologians, see above on CB 77 and 78. In a letter to Chanut of 20 November 1647, Descartes also mentions the dangers of calumny in connection with his reluctance to write on morals; he adds the comment that attempts to regulate the morality of others should, in any case, be left to sovereigns or their agents (AT v. 87). This remark confirms the reliability of Burman's reporting here at CB 80, on Descartes' attitude to ethics. See however RODIS-LEWIS, for an attempt to endow Descartes with a major interest in moral philosophy.

CB 81. By introducing this text from the *Discourse*, Burman brings Descartes back to the thorny problem of the Circle, which has already been discussed at CB 6. For Descartes' important additional comments here, see Introduction, pp. xxx ff.

CB 82. l. 11: simply as it is now. Descartes does not mean that the philosopher should ignore the past history and evolution of phenomena—on the contrary (see above on CB 58). The point, rather, is that the scientist cannot deal with events requiring a supernatural explanation (e.g. the situation of mankind before the flood; lines 3 ff.); his subject is the *natural* world—the world 'as it is now'. There is a closely similar passage at CB 32, line 6 ff. where, again, the contrast is with supernatural matters.

ll. 13/14. human life could be prolonged. In the *Discourse*, the value of science is closely linked to its potentiality for benefiting mankind; the preservation of health, in particular (both physical and mental), is described as the 'chief blessing and foundation of all other blessings in life' (AT vi. 62). In his own case, Descartes admitted that he looked after himself 'as carefully as a rich man with gout' (to Mersenne, AT ii. 480). His careful diet is referred to by the Abbé Picot, who stayed with him at his Egmond retreat for three months in 1647; according to Picot, Descartes was convinced that he was on the way to discovering the secret which would enable men to live to an age of three or four hundred (reported in Baillet's *Vie de Mr. Des Cartes*: see AT xi. 671).

ll. 25/6. nature still remains the same. Because it is a 'machine' which works in accordance with universal mathematical laws (cf. CB 45). But Descartes is skating over some difficulties here, since he himself admits at CB 45 that the messages which the body sends to the mind in illness (e.g. in the case of a dropsical man with a raging thirst) may be highly misleading.

ll. 34/5. with her perfect internal awareness (*sui optima conscia*). There is a strong parallel here with Descartes' attitude to our mental endowments. Just as the *lux naturalis* will get us further than all the inherited 'wisdom' of the past, so the body can look after itself better than 'les plus savants docteurs' (cf. AT iv. 330). It is remarkable, however, to find Descartes using the term 'aware' (*conscia*) of nature—i.e. the machine of the body, which is of course pure extension—even though he is talking loosely and metaphorically.

ll. 44/5. Tiberius Caesar said (or Cato, I think). Tiberius is the right answer: the source for his success in doing without a physician is the biography of Suetonius: 'valitudine prosperrima usus est, tempore quidem principatus paene toto illaesa, quamvis a trigesimo aetatis anno arbitratu eam suo rexerit sine adiumento consiliove medicorum' (*Vita Tiberii*, 68). I am inclined to think that the alternative attribution (to Cato) was subsequently added by Burman or the copyist; Descartes makes a similar remark about health in a letter to Newcastle of October 1645, and there it is Tiberius who is referred to, without any doubt or hesitation (AT iv. 329).

l. 48. be his own doctor. On this relaxed and optimistic note the *Conversation* closes. Descartes' cheery confidence in do-it-yourself medicine assumes, in retrospect, a poignant touch of irony. Though just turned fifty-two, he has less than two years to live.

Amsterdam, 20 April 1648. For the place and date, which differ from those given at the beginning of the MS., see Introduction, pp. x ff.

CONSPECTUS OF THE TEXT

Column 1: CB number (present edition).
Column 2: page reference to standard Latin text in AT v.
Column 3: Latin rubric: key words from Descartes' text quoted by
      Burman.
Column 4: brief description of topics covered.

CB	AT v.	Rubric	Topics
MEDIT. I			
1	146	vel a sensibus vel per sensus	sensory and innate knowledge; the 'prephilosophical' mind; axioms and scepticism
2	147	Supponam igitur	} malignant demon
3	147	summe potentem	
4	147	ex nullo syllogismo	the Cogito
5	147/8	in quod non potest ferri summum ens	God and deception; memory
6	148/9	denique quod circulum	Cartesian Circle; nature of thought and the mind; eternity
7	149	Quod autem nihil in mente	} thought and consciousness
8	149	a cogitatione dependens	
9	149/50	Quamobrem non dubito	the mind never without thought; mental activity of infants; intellectual memory
MEDIT. II			
10	150/1	et si fas est dicere malignum	malignant demon
11	151	is qui me creavit	author of our being— doubt
12	151	tum quid ea sit	} substance and accidents
13	151	neque enim abstraxi	(wax)
14	151/2	adaequat infinitam Dei potestatem	adequate knowledge
MEDIT. III			
15	152	vix mihi ullam	material falsity in ideas
16	152	forte etiam	nature of the mind as gradually discovered in first three Meditations

CB	AT v.	Rubric	Topics
17	152/3	nullum plane habebo	order of discovery *v.* order of exposition
18	153	et quia nullae ideae nisi tantum rei [tamquam rerum] esse possunt	'ideas'
19	153	qua enim ratione intelligerem me dubitare	perfection; 'priority' of positive over negative
20	154	non possim ejus ope	knowledge and power
21	154	nulla differentia [difficiliora] factu mihi videntur	understanding, conception and imagination; 'indefinite' and 'infinite'
22	154/5	majus est creare vel conservare subjectum quam attributa	substance and attributes
23	155/6	tamquam si inde sequeretur	creation and eternity
24	156	{ valde credibile est propius tamen est	cause and effect
25	156	omnis res cui inest	substance and attributes; substrate
26	156	aliquod idolum	idols and material falsity
27	157	sed me istam vim	proof of perfect being
28	157	de idea angeli	angels and 'res cogitans'

MEDIT. IV

CB	AT v.	Rubric	Topics
29	158	{ atque ob hanc unicam rationem nec fingi potest	final causes
30	158	ex hoc ipso quod ejus ideam formare possim	idea of perfection
31	158/9	non tamen in se formaliter	understanding and will; perfection of human will
32	159	possum tamen illo altero	freedom and indifference; original sin
33	159/60	cujus idea in intellectu divine prius fuerit	God as source of possibility as well as actuality

MEDIT. V

CB	AT v.	Rubric	Topics
34	160	ut patet ex eo	true and real *v.* fictitious objects; difference between Mathematics and Physics

CB	AT v.	Rubric	Topics
35	161	non possum duos ant plures ejusmodi Deos intellegere	uniqueness of God
36	164	quia sumus [tam] assueti	distinction between essence and existence
37	161	nec in ulla re	'ideas' and 'things'—contradiction can arise in ideas alone
38	161	nec ulla umquam in claris et distinctis esse potest	no contradiction possible in clear and distinct ideas
39	161/2	ac proinde	perfection and priority (triangle)

MEDIT. VI

CB	AT v.	Rubric	Topics
40	162	illas existere	⎫ imagination
41	162	quamvis illa [a me] abesset	⎭
42	162/3	ad illud velut inspiciendum	imagination *v.* perception
43	163	Et primo quoniam	mind and body
44	163	arctissimo esse conjunctum et quasi permixtum	interaction between mind and body
45	163/4	longe melius est	human error; the body a machine
46	164	nulla cum profunditate spectatur	'surface' (*superficies*)
47	164	quorum extremitates sunt simul	'contiguous' and 'continuous'
48	165	*Observandum*	The *Meditations*; relation of Metaphysics to Physics

[*Notae in programma*]

CB	AT v.	Rubric	Topics
49	165	*In Resp. ad Prog.*	innate ideas

Principia Philosophiae
LIB. I

CB	AT v.	Rubric	Topics
50	165/6	ita ut per unicam	God identical with his decrees; divine 'immutability'; necessity and indifference; Gomarists and Arminians

CB	AT v.	Rubric	Topics
51	167	indefinitum	'infinite' and 'indefinite'
52	167	tamquam aeternas veritates	eternal truths v. contingent truths

LIB. II

53	167	clare videre nobis videmur	'appearance' and the external world
54	168	aquae ab eo sublevatae gravitas et ejusdem lentor	motion and rest: movement of a ship
55	168	saepe sit valde contorta	complex motion (carriage wheel)
56	168	Prima	French edition of *Principles*

LIB. III

57	168	propter nos solos	dangers of anthropocentric cosmology
58	168/9	creatus cum omni sua perfectione	the creation: Descartes' view of Genesis
59	170	motusque habent aliquo modo circulares	circular motion of particles
60	170	magnitudine mediocres	the three 'elements'
61	170/1	circa alia quaedam puncta	scientific hypothesis
62	171	quia quo minima	
63	173	plus habent superficiei	ratio between surface area and mass
64	171	dividuntur vero secundum molem	
65	171	pro tertio	the three 'heavens'; our own world not centre of universe but simply a planet
66	172	sed tantummodo in pressione	nature of light
67	172	*Art. 66*	'mathematics' and 'mechanics'; utility of models
68	172	non esse inter se aequales	vortexes: inter-stellar distances
69	172	angustius e regione centri	vortexes
70	173	ut enim videmus turbinem	vortexes: comparison of the top
71	173	ipsamque impellit	rotation of earth: balloon analogy

CB	*AT v.*	*Rubric*	*Topics*
LIB. IV			
72	173/4	talis propensio non sit tanta	Descartes' theory of gravity
73	174	in aequipondio consistere	'mechanics' and machines
74	174	in tria praecipua genera	terrestrial matter— three types of shape
75	174/5	supra aliud oblique ducitur	nature of glass

ex *Dissertatione de Methodo*

76	175	abundare se putat	'good sense'—universal endowment
77	175	ad logicam	'Logic' *v.* 'Dialectic'
78	176	eodem pacto se mutuo sequi	Philosophy and Theology
79	176/7	assuefacerem ingenium meum veritati agnoscendae	importance of Mathematics in Descartes' philosophy; Algebra; imagination in Mathematics and Physics; Mathematics and Metaphysics
80	178	non pigebit adscribere	Descartes' attitude to ethics
81	178	sed si nesciremus	Cartesian circle
82	178/9	fortassis a senectutis debilitatione	Philosophy *v.* Theology; prolongation of life; 'natural' medicine

BIBLIOGRAPHY

Note: The following is simply a list of works referred to in the Introduction and Commentary. A full bibliography covering all the issues discussed in the *Conversation* would occupy a whole volume. Such a volume is the invaluable SEBBA. A selection of the more important recent Cartesian literature may be found in DONEY (1) and KENNY (1).

ADAM, C., *Descartes, Entretien avec Burman*, texte présenté, traduit et annoté (Paris: Boivin, 1937).

ANSCOMBE, G. E. M., 'Substance', *Proceedings of the Aristotelian Society*, supp. vol. XXXVIII (1964), pp. 7–78.

ARMSTRONG, D. M., *A Materialist Theory of the Mind* (London: Routledge, 1968).

AUSTIN, J. L., *Sense and Sensibilia* (Oxford: Clarendon Press, 1962).

BECK, L. J., *The Method of Descartes. A Study of the Regulae* (Oxford: Clarendon Press, 1952).

BRIDOUX, A., *Œuvres et lettres de Descartes* (Paris: Gallimard, 1953).

CHOMSKY, N., *Language and Mind* (New York: Harcourt Brace & World, 1968).

CLAUBERG, J., *Paraphrasis in Renati Des Cartes Meditationes* (Duisberg: Wyngaerden, 1658).

COLLINS, J., 'Descartes' Philosophy of Nature', *American Philosophical Quarterly Monograph* (Oxford: Blackwell, 1971).

DONEY, W. (1) (ed.), *Descartes. A Collection of Critical Essays* (London: Macmillan, 1968).

——(2), 'The Cartesian Circle', *Journal of the History of Ideas*, vol. XVI (1955), pp. 324–38.

EWING, A. C., *A Short Commentary on Kant's Critique of Pure Reason* (London: Methuen, 1938).

FRANKFURT, H. G., *Demons, Dreamers and Madmen, The defence of reason in Descartes' Meditations* (New York: Bobbs-Merrill, 1970).

GEWIRTH, A., 'Clearness and Distinctness in Descartes', *Philosophy*, vol. XVIII (1943), pp. 17–36.

GIBSON, A. B., *The Philosophy of Descartes* (London: Methuen, 1932).

GILSON, E. (1), *Index Scolastico-Cartésien* (Paris: Alcan, 1913).

——(2), *René Descartes, Discours de la Méthode*, texte et commentaire par Étienne Gilson (Paris: Vrin, 1925).

——(3), *La Doctrine Cartésienne de la Liberté et la Théologie* (Paris: Alcan, 1913).

HARRÉ, R., *The Philosophies of Science* (London: Oxford University Press, 1972).

HUME, David, *A Treatise of Human Nature* and *An Enquiry Concerning Human Understanding*, ed. L. A. Selby-Bigge (Oxford: Clarendon Press, 1896 and 1902).

KENNY, A. (1), *Descartes. A Study of his Philosophy* (New York: Random House, 1968).

——(2), 'Descartes on the Will', in R. J. Butler (ed.), *Cartesian Studies* (Oxford: Blackwell, 1972).

LEIBNIZ, G. W., *Die Philosophischen Schriften von G. W. Leibniz*, ed. C. I. Gerhardt (7 vols., Berlin: Weidmann, 1875–90).

LOCKE, J., *An Essay Concerning Human Understanding*, ed. J. W. Yolton (London: Dent, 1961).

MALCOLM, N., 'Descartes' Proof that his Essence is Thinking', *Philosophical Review*, vol. LXXIV (1965), pp. 315–38. Reprinted in DONEY (1), pp. 313–37.

MOORE, G. E., *Principia Ethica* (Cambridge: Cambridge University Press, 1903, repr. 1962).

POPKIN, R. H., *The History of Scepticism, from Erasmus to Descartes* (New York: Harper & Row, 1968).

RODIS-LEWIS, G., *La Morale de Descartes* (Paris: Presses Universitaires de France, 1957).

RUSSELL, B., *The Problems of Philosophy* (repr. London: Oxford University Press, 1967).

SEBBA, G., *Bibliographica Cartesiana* (The Hague: Nijhoff, 1964).

SMITH, N. Kemp (trans.), *Immanuel Kant's Critique of Pure Reason* (London: Macmillan, 1929).

THIJSSEN-SCHOUTE, G. C. Louise, *Nederlands Cartesianisme* (Amsterdam: N.V. Noord-Hollandsche Uitgevers Maatschappij, 1954).

VROOMAN, J. R., *René Descartes. A Biography* (New York: Putnam, 1970).

WILLIAMS, B., 'Descartes', in P. Edwards (ed.), *The Encyclopaedia of Philosophy* (New York: Macmillan, 1967).

INDEX

TABLE OF PASSAGES FROM DESCARTES' WORKS DISCUSSED IN THE CONVERSATION

Discourse on the Method

Part I	AT vi. 1 and 540, HR i. 81: CB 76			
Part II	17	549	91	77
	19	550	92	78, 79
Part III	22	552	95	80
Part IV	33	559	102	19
	39	562	105	81
Part VI	62	575	120	82

Meditations

First Meditation	AT vii. 18, HR i. 145: CB 1		
	22	148	2, 3
Second Meditation	26	151	10
	29	153	11
	32	156	12
Third Meditation	37	160	15
	39	161	16
	42	163	17
	44	164	18
	45	166	19
	47	167	20
	48	168	21, 23
	51	170	24
Fourth Meditation	55	173	29
	57	174	30, 31
	61	178	32
Fifth Meditation	64	180	34
	68	182	35
Sixth Meditation	71	185	40
	73	186	41, 42
	78	190	42, 43
	81	192	44
	89	198	45

Notes against a Programme
AT viiib. 358: CB 49

Principles of Philosophy

	art	AT viii.	HR i.	CB
Book I	10	8,	222:	4
	23	14	228	50
	26	15	230	51
	48	22	238	52
Book II	1	41	254	53
	26	55	—	54
	32	58	—	55
	46	68	—	56
Book III	2	81	271	57
	45	99	—	58
	46	100	—	59, 60, 61
	50	104	—	62, 63, 64
	53	106	—	65
	63	115	—	66
	66	117	—	67
	68	119	—	68
	83	138	—	69
	144	194	—	70
	150	198	—	71
Book IV	23	213	—	72
	27	216	—	73
	33	220	—	74
	125	270	—	75

Replies to Objections

	AT vii.	HR ii.	CB
First Replies	116,	19:	36
Second Replies	138	37	28
	139	37	26, 27
	140	38	4
	152	46	37, 38
	161	53	25
	166	57	22
Fourth Replies	220	97	14
	245	114	6
	246	115	7, 8, 9
Fifth Replies	359	212	13
	373	222	24
	375	223	29
	382	227	39
Sixth Replies	428	245	5
	432	248	33
	433	249	46, 47